PALM SPRINGS
GOLF

PALM SPRINGS
GOLF

A History of Coachella Valley Legends & Fairways

LARRY BOHANNAN

THE
History
PRESS

Published by The History Press
Charleston, SC 29403
www.historypress.net

First published 2015

Manufactured in the United States

ISBN 978.1.62619.963.7

Library of Congress Control Number: 2015936857

Contents

Acknowledgements

If you want to find out how many friends you have, or how many you can make, try to write a book.

For me, writing this book brought me back to several old friends who helped on this project, and it gave me a chance to meet and work with new people who I hope I can work with more in the future.

New friends include Jeri Vogelsong, director of the Palm Springs Historical Society, who helped with photos and stories. The same is true of the staff at La Quinta Historical Society, especially Jill-Lynn Nunemaker, who was patient with my requests and my stories.

Jennie Kays, head librarian at the Palm Springs Library, helped with access to digital newspapers as well as suggestions of where else to sleuth.

Old friends include people at the desert's two biggest golf courses who were generous with their photo archives. That includes Bob Marra and Pat Bennett at Desert Classic Charities, the nonprofit that runs the desert's PGA Tour event, which is even without an official name as I write this. And there is Gabe Codding of International Management Group and the tournament director of the ANA Inspiration on the LPGA. Gabe was also generous with access to his photo archives.

Thunderbird Country Club has a wonderful archive of old photos from its storied history. Nick DeKock helped me go through looking for treasures. And Graeme Baxter showed that he has a talent for more than just the wonderful oil paintings that grace the clubhouses and homes of professional golfers throughout the world. He is also a talented photographer who allowed me to use some of those images.

Acknowledgements

And there were those who were generous with their time in sharing their stories and remembrances, like Andy Vossler, Marlene Hagge, Bill Bone, Amy Alcott and Al Geiberger.

Finally, there is Megan Laddusaw of The History Press, who somehow had the faith to approach me about this book and who tolerated the fact that after more than thirty years in the newspaper business, I tend to only work hard when a deadline is looming. She kept this project on pace, for which I am grateful.

Introduction

I've always joked that one reason I love the history of the Coachella Valley is that it wasn't all that long ago.

Honestly, the history of golf in Palm Springs and the surrounding area isn't quite like trying to memorize the history of, say, the Old Course at St. Andrews in Scotland. Golf first appeared in the Coachella Valley in the 1920s, so when I first started playing golf in the area in 1982, the game was less than sixty years old in the desert. That was just three generations from the first golf holes to the booming development era of the 1980s.

And while I didn't know some of the great names in golf in the area, like Johnny Dawson, Milt Hicks or Helen Dettweiler, it was easy to find people who did know those great names well as I began covering golf for the *Desert Sun* newspaper in 1986.

But even in such a short period of time, it was difficult for a history buff like me to get completely accurate information about some of the desert courses from years ago. Depending on the reference and historical books you read, Thomas O'Donnell's golf course in Palm Springs, the oldest existing course in the Coachella Valley, opened anywhere from 1923 to 1934. The evidence is clear that the course was being played in 1927. The Hotel La Quinta course that opened in 1927 gets little mention in the area's history books. And the Mashie Course at the Desert Inn was having a wall built around it in 1924, despite some claims that those holes didn't open until 1926. I was always stunned to meet people who had no idea the desert had hosted two Ryder Cups in the 1950s.

Still, nailing down the timeline of when this course or that course opened was never the intent of this book, though the chronology of the game's growth was important. Instead, I wanted to talk about the people and personalities who drove the growth of the game in the Coachella Valley. The personalities who made golf part of the very fabric of the desert were often larger than life. People like Bob Hope, Bing Crosby, Arnold Palmer, Johnny Dawson, Dwight Eisenhower and Dinah Shore also reflected how golf in the Coachella Valley was different from the game played anywhere else. Other golf areas had top pros but not celebrities. Some areas had celebrities but not top players. Some areas had top pros and celebrities, but who had Arnold Palmer, Bob Hope and a few past presidents of the United States for some spice?

By the 1990s, the Coachella Valley had more televised golf events annually than any other area of the country, a combination of the celebrities, the pros, the compelling desert courses and the near-perfect weather and scenery. It was an amazing ascent from a collection of flat holes in the middle of the desert dunes seventy years earlier. It has all made for a fascinating history, one that I have studied as a job and as a hobby since I first came to the desert. It's a history that I hope continues to add chapters for another century.

CHAPTER 1
Some Grass for the Desert Dunes

B ob Hope, certainly one of the most famous residents in the history of Palm Springs and the surrounding Coachella Valley, loved to skewer his friends who shared his famous passion for golf. And perhaps Hope's favorite target was a fairly famous resident of the Southern California desert himself, former president Gerald Ford.

Gerald Ford is the person who made golf a contact sport. Gerald Ford's game has improved, though, because he is only hitting Democrats these days.

But one of Hope's favorite slaps at his close friend Ford was that you never know which golf course Gerald Ford is playing until Ford tees off.

Hope's comment was inspired by the former president's tendency to let loose with wayward shots that would land in the wrong fairway or hit an innocent bystander in the gallery of the numerous tournaments Ford would play. Ford actually wasn't a bad golfer, but few double-digit handicappers play in front of galleries that line both sides of the fairway.

But Hope's zinger said as much about the area where Hope and Ford lived as it did about Ford's game. The Coachella Valley, a desert area about two hours east of Los Angeles, is as famous for its connection to golf courses and professional golf as it is for its connection with high-profile residents like Hope, Ford and Frank Sinatra. In fact, at the corner of Bob Hope Drive and Frank Sinatra Drive in Rancho Mirage, one of the nine cities in the Coachella Valley, it is possible to hit three different golf courses with a well-struck drive. Add a couple 3-woods to the end of that drive and you can reach another four golf courses.

In all, a desert that at the turn of the twentieth century seemed like an inhospitable place for pioneer settlers, much less recreational golfers, is the home to more than 120 golf courses. More than a dozen states have fewer courses.

A garden of fairways in a dry, hot desert? To understand the importance of golf in the Coachella Valley and how the sport gained a grip on the area, it's important to understand how the Coachella Valley was positioned to grow into a resort community at all.

What would become a golfer's paradise in the second half of the twentieth century was the home of the Cahuilla Indians for thousands of years. In the second half of the 1800s, the rest of the world began to encroach on the Cahuillas' land. Railroads were bringing more and more of modern civilization to the West Coast of the United States, and that included California and the Coachella Valley, about 120 miles east of Los Angeles. By the 1870s, the Southern Pacific Railroad was building a line out of Los Angeles through the Coachella Valley and the Cahuilla land. In a deal for the land, the federal government produced a checkerboard pattern of land for the area, giving the Cahuillas every other square mile. It never dawned on anyone that, years later, one of those square miles would be right in the middle of Palm Springs.

In the 1890s, the United States Department of Agriculture began experiments with growing dates from plants that had been imported from the Middle East. Some initial success inspired a USDA horticulturist named Bernard Johnson to begin growing date trees that had been imported from Algeria. Date farms became a key part of the Coachella Valley's burgeoning agricultural industry and spread throughout desert. With a railway to ship the dates across the country, agriculture in the desert began to thrive.

And it would continue to thrive, thanks to a secret hidden below the sand, desert brush and rocky golden and red mountains that ringed the valley. It was a secret the Cahuillas knew and one that would make golf possible in such an inhospitable land. Beneath the desert was water.

Not just water, but literally trillions of gallons of water in an aquifer that could easily be reached from the surface through artesian wells. In the eastern part of the Coachella Valley, water could be found by digging no more than a foot deep in some places. The aquifer is described by the Coachella Valley Water District as a bathtub filled with sand and rocks, with water filling the spaces in between.

Many Indians had walk-in wells, where they would walk down no more than a dozen steps and fetch water in clay jars. It would take the white settlers a little while to discover the ease of reaching water in the desert, but once they did, development was not far behind. Water meant people could survive in the desert in the winters, even though the hot, dry summers with temperatures over 110 degrees on a regular basis made the area a winter haven to be avoided in the summer.

While the railroad and agriculture were growing in the eastern part of the Coachella Valley in areas like Coachella, Mecca and Indio, it was a desire for health that was bringing white settlers to the western part of the valley in the late 1800s. The desert's warm weather combined with the arid environment and natural hot springs began attracting those looking for relief from respiratory ailments like tuberculosis and asthma. The names of the early settlers, names like McCallum, Murray and Coffman, still dot the desert today on streets, buildings and schools.

Nellie Coffman and her husband, Dr. Harry Coffman, opened a sanitarium for those with respiratory diseases in Palm Springs in 1908. Eventually, Harry Coffman left to open another sanitarium farther south and east in the desert, but Nellie stayed in Palm Springs with her two sons, George Roberson and

In this 1930 photo from the terrace of Thomas O'Donnell's home, the Mashie Course at the Desert Inn can be seen. The Mashie Course existed until the 1950s, with the Desert Inn lasting until the 1960s. *Courtesy of Palm Springs Historical Society. All rights reserved.*

Earl Coffman. Nellie had already decided that there could be more money in taking care of the healthy rather than the sick and turned her Desert Inn into a bungalow getaway that attracted the rich and famous. Nellie's stock in trade was home-style hospitality, the kind that would get customers to come back time and again to the little bungalows in the center of what was known as the village.

Mother Coffman, as Nellie became known through the Coachella Valley, wanted to offer her guests everything they could ask for. By 1924, the Desert Inn was established as a destination for movie stars, government officials and some of the richest businessmen in the nation who were discovering the desert. A few short golf holes sprang up between the bungalows of the hotel. The holes required, in some cases, no more than a well-struck wedge to reach the roughed-out greens on the grass of the property. Thus was born the Mashie Course, mashie being a common golf term at the time for what today would be called a 5-iron. It was short and sporty, without, perhaps, much more thought of design than filling the spaces between Coffman's bungalows and a nearby meadow. A report in the *Banning Record* newspaper in November 1924 stated, "The Desert Inn golf course is being surrounded by a substantial stone wall, making a beautiful effect against the hillside."

It was a start for golf in the desert, a start that one of Mother Coffman's frequent guests thought he could improve on. Thomas O'Donnell was

Overlooking the Desert Inn's Mashie Course, with plenty of desert to the east of the village of Palm Springs in 1927. *Courtesy of Palm Springs Historical Society. All rights reserved.*

The rock wall in the foreground was a famous boundary for the Desert Inn, one of the earliest Palm Springs hotels and the site of the Mashie Course. *Courtesy of Palm Springs Historical Society. All rights reserved.*

more than just a wealthy man. He was, in fact, one of the richest men in California, known as one of the Big Four in the California oil industry in the early part of the twentieth century. In the early 1900s, O'Donnell had worked for other companies in the oil fields of Long Beach and then set off as an independent driller and speculator. He was so successful in establishing and leading companies that O'Donnell could pretty much do anything he wanted financially and live anywhere he wanted. He decided that Palm Springs was for him, but with a few changes.

Like so many before him, O'Donnell came to the Coachella Valley for his health, with the clean, dry air helping his respiratory problems. He would stay at the Desert Inn, and he and Nellie Coffman became friends from his frequent visits. O'Donnell would hit balls on the Mashie Course, but he wanted to satisfy his love of the game.

When Coffman approached O'Donnell for a loan so that she could transform the Desert Inn into a bigger and better Spanish-style hotel, the two old friends struck a deal. In return for the money Coffman needed, Coffman agreed to lease about fifteen acres of land adjoining the Desert Inn for a permanent home for O'Donnell and his wife, an osteopath named Dr. Winifred Willis. Coffman agreed to oversee the building of

That famous O'Donnell House high above the village of Palm Springs was where oilman Thomas O'Donnell lived above his famous golf course. The house was known as El Ojo del Desierto, or the Eye of the Desert. *Courtesy of Palm Springs Historical Society. All rights reserved.*

O'Donnell's new home, and she would have the money to expand the Desert Inn.

The home, known as *El Ojo del Desierto*, or the Eye of the Desert, was built up into the foothills of the San Jacinto Mountains and became the highest structure in the desert. But O'Donnell was hardly done putting his imprint on Palm Springs. There was still the love he and his wife had for golf. So below his famed desert home, O'Donnell bought two pieces of property that combined for just over thirty-four acres. And then he set about planning his own private nine-hole course.

How does an oilman design his own golf course? O'Donnell would do the job himself, with the help of a group of friends, including John Kline, who would eventually manage the golf property. In his February 23, 1945 obituary in the *Desert Sun* newspaper, O'Donnell's design concept was explained. It was simple and yet perfectly sensible: "Using a driver, then an iron, he marked the spot where the ball stopped for the first green. This followed with all the clubs in his bag until he had the nine-hole course plotted."

Of course, his golf course, as well as the rest of the village of Palm Springs, needed water. With the underground aquifer still a bit of a mystery to the original settlers, O'Donnell and a group of his friends brought water fourteen miles from an area called Whitewater Canyon, located north and west of Palm Springs. The Whitewater Mutual Water Company would play a part in the early development of the village, even with the development of a third golf course a few years later.

As O'Donnell was building his golf course in 1926, another man at the opposite end of the Coachella Valley was planning a similar venture at what would become one of the most iconic spots in the desert.

Walter H. Morgan, a well-to-do San Francisco businessman, had fallen in love with the desert in the eastern half of the Coachella Valley and its tranquil, serene nature. The area was mostly sand dunes and was heavy with agriculture, including the date farms.

Morgan saw an opportunity to build something that could capture the desert in it simplest form. To begin his plan, Morgan formed the Desert Development Company and acquired 1,400 acres from the Cahuilla Indians in an area twenty miles from Palm Springs. Access to the area was on paved roads like Highway 111 and Highway 99 (along what is now U.S. Interstate 10), but it was still dirt roads back ten or so miles to the south to get to Morgan's land.

Along with Los Angeles architect Gordon Kaufmann, Morgan envisioned a small retreat with six Spanish-style adobe haciendas with tile roofs, along with a dining room and a lobby. Total cost of the construction was said to be $150,000.

But the area for Morgan's hideaway had no real name. An area known as Happy Point at the base of the Santa Rosa Mountains was more than two miles away. Indio, a growing community of its own, was more than eight miles to the northwest. And this certainly wasn't Palm Springs.

Morgan settled on calling his desert retreat the Hotel La Quinta. First-year Spanish students know that *la quinta* means "the fifth." But it also can refer to a retreat, hacienda or resting place. And that is what Morgan saw for his Hotel La Quinta, which was built like a Spanish hacienda with bungalows for the individual rooms. Eventually, La Quinta grew to mean the community in and around the hotel, and it was the name given to the city when it incorporated in 1982.

The hotel itself opened on December 15, 1926, but a grand opening didn't come until January 29, 1927. The hotel became an immediate hit, especially among the rich and famous from Hollywood who were looking for a little quiet and seclusion in their lives. And at nearly twenty miles beyond Palm Springs, the Hotel La Quinta offered a different kind of getaway from the hotels popping up in Palm Springs like the Desert Inn.

Seclusion is one thing, but visitors still wanted some entertainment at the Hotel La Quinta. The hotel offered tennis, croquet and horseback riding. But golf was growing in popularity, and it was a long trek along dirt and paved roads from the Hotel La Quinta into Palm Springs to play the Mashie Course. So Morgan decided that a nine-hole course would be perfect for his retreat.

The nine-hole course was built throughout 1926. A notice in the February 25, 1927 edition of *La Quinta Hotel Legend*, a kind of in-house newsletter for the hotel, included a small notice under the banner "Announcement." It read, "The opening to the public of the Golf Course in connection with the new Hotel La Quinta. A maintenance fee of one dollar per person per day will be made as 'Green Fee.' Golf Clubs will be available for rental at a nominal fee. Also, saddle horses for hire."

That means the Hotel La Quinta course opened a few months before the O'Donnell course, and the desert now had golf courses at both ends of the Coachella Valley: the Hotel La Quinta course for guests and the public, the Mashie Course for guests at the Desert Inn and Thomas O'Donnell's golf course, which was for his private use. But the truth was O'Donnell never really kept the course to himself. For the first few years it was open, O'Donnell's course produced little fanfare or headlines because it truly was a private course for him and his friends, along with guests at the Desert Inn. By 1932, though, O'Donnell had opened his golf course at times to the public and to some famous visitors. Those who played discovered the quirky design features of O'Donnell's layout, like a par-three fifth hole with a blind shot played over the point of the nearby mountain and seventh and eighth holes that play across each other's paths.

Through the next two decades, O'Donnell would be one of the desert's greatest benefactors. He allowed his course to be used for a variety of activities other than golf, and the fact that his course existed brought even more famous people to the desert. It was common to see Hollywood names like Bob Hope, Bing Crosby and the radio team of Amos and Andy, Freeman Gosden and Charles Correl, playing O'Donnell's course. In addition, O'Donnell's generosity helped with the construction of a public library and a community health clinic.

While O'Donnell came to the desert first for a respiratory issue, it was heart issues that eventually made it impossible for him to make the climb up the hills to get to his famed Ojo del Desierto home. He built a second home on the edge of his golf course on the desert floor, and there he would sit and watch his friends and the village in general play the golf course.

Charles Correll and Freeman Gosden, who formed the famous radio team of *Amos 'n' Andy*, at O'Donnell Golf Club in the 1930s. The pair, with Gosden playing Amos and Correll as Andy, broadcast their radio show from Palm Springs' El Mirador Hotel in the early 1930s. *Courtesy of Palm Springs Historical Society. All rights reserved.*

By 1944, with his health failing, O'Donnell decided to deed his golf course to the city of Palm Springs. But to make sure the golf course remained a golf course, he set up a ninety-nine-year lease for a group of his friends who would oversee the course. The Committee of Twenty-five took over the lease just a few months before O'Donnell's death at age seventy-four. That lease remains intact to this day.

With water now coming into the village and with the most famous people in Hollywood visiting the area, from Charlie Chaplin to Buddy Rogers and Albert Einstein to William Randolph Hearst, Palm Springs seemed to be crying out for a bigger, more luxurious hotel. The answer would come in 1928 with the construction of El Mirador Hotel.

Leading the group of investors by purchasing twenty acres just north of the village and construction of the grand hotel was Prescott Stevens. Stevens had made his money as a cattle baron in Colorado, but he was the latest businessman and developer to become smitten with the quiet charms of Palm Springs. Stevens is reported himself to have invested $1 million in

El Mirador Hotel, with its famous tower, was a landmark in early Palm Springs and the site of a nine-hole golf course in the late 1920s and early 1930s. It became an army hospital during World War II. *Courtesy of Palm Springs Historical Society. All rights reserved.*

the two-hundred-room El Mirador project, which included a sixty-foot bell tower that practically became the symbol of the city.

When Stevens came to the desert, his chauffer was an African American man who was born in New Orleans, Lawrence Crossley. Crossley turned out to be far more than a chauffeur, though. He was an investor in the hotel and in the Whitewater Mutual Water Company. He bought land and developed it in the area. And, or so the story goes, Crossley was the man who either designed a nine-hole golf course attached to the hotel or redesigned the course after its first season.

The course opened in February 1929, just two months after El Mirador itself opened with a grand New Year's Eve party. The El Mirador course started with a 500-yard par-five, but the nine-hole course played to just 2,816 yards and a par-thirty-five for men and thirty-nine for women.

The golf course was only part of what attracted visitors to El Mirador. Tennis courts and swimming pools also brought Hollwood to the desert. But the appeal of the golf course, the swimming pool and the tennis courts couldn't overcome the stock market crash of October 1929. Stevens and his investment partners were hit hard by the crash, and within just a few years, they had to sell their magnificent palace. The golf course, in the windiest part of the desert at the time, the exposed north end of the village,

A shirtless golfer putts out on one of the greens of the El Mirador Hotel golf course in the early 1930s. The course struggled to remain open as the hotel's owners struggled with the Great Depression. *Courtesy of Palm Springs Historical Society. All rights reserved.*

struggled as well and would eventually be abandoned and swallowed up by the desert.

Before the course disappeared, and with the Palm Springs area growing in popularity with the Hollywood crowd, it only made sense that golf, Palm Springs and Hollywood came together for the first time. In 1930, a caravan of more than two hundred actors and technicians descended on El Mirador Hotel and its golf course to film parts of the Paramount Pictures movie *Follow Thru*. Based on an English play, the ninety-minute Technicolor musical comedy revolves around a top female golfer who loses a big match. After the loss, she employs a new teaching pro with whom she falls in love. The part of the teaching pro was portrayed by one of Hollywood's biggest stars, Charles "Buddy" Rogers. Rogers had starred in *Wings*, the first Academy Award winner for Best Picture, just three years earlier. He would later become an avid golfer himself and a desert resident at Thunderbird Country Club with his wife, fellow early Hollywood star Mary Pickford.

And so the game of golf and Hollywood had put down roots in the Coachella Valley, roots that would grow stronger and tighter over the coming decades. But while the stage was set for golf to become a vital part of the desert, it would be another two decades before the game propelled the desert to new heights.

CHAPTER 2
The World Discovers the Desert

The Coachella Valley was still a sleepy little desert village as the 1930s began. Officially, Palm Springs was not a city yet, and the U.S. census for 1930 listed just 1,450 residents. The town virtually shut down in the summer with no air conditioning to keep hotel rooms comfortable in the 110-degree-plus temperatures.

But a culture was growing around the many desert hotels that had opened in the 1910s and 1920s, featuring names like the Desert Inn, the El Mirador Hotel and the Del Tahquitz. And sports were certainly part of that culture.

The 1930s saw major swimming competitions at the pool at El Mirador, plans for a massive polo facility at that same hotel and tennis exhibitions by some of the biggest names in the sport like Don Budge, Fred Perry and Ellsworth Vines, as well as small tournaments at the Desert Inn or the new and popular Racquet Club, founded by actors Ralph Bellamy and Charlie Farrell. Golf wouldn't be left out.

Perhaps the first true breakthrough for the Coachella Valley in terms of being nationally recognized as a golfing destination came in February 1935, just a few years after the desert saw its first four courses spring up from the sandy dunes. A professional golf tournament was coming to the village of Palm Springs.

Set for the nine-hole O'Donnell Golf Course, which was also known as the Desert Golf Club, the tournament featured a gaudy purse of $2,000 for the twenty-one players in the field, although a few familiar local amateurs would also participate in the event.

This 1928 aerial shot of the village of Palm Springs shows snowcapped Mount San Jacinto. In the right foreground is El Mirador Hotel's golf course under construction for a 1929 opening. *Courtesy of Palm Springs Historical Society. All rights reserved.*

"We have received word from Walter Hagen, noted professional, that the golfers invited have accepted the invitations, and we expect the tournament to be an outstanding one," said Harold Hicks, president of the junior chamber of commerce for Palm Springs and a member of one of the village's founding families.

The tournament was organized and conducted by the local junior chamber, and the purse and other costs were underwritten by local residents and businesses that, as the weekly *Desert Sun* newspaper reported, "see in the tournament a splendid opportunity to obtain nationwide publicity for Palm Springs and to establish this resort and its courses on the 'winter golf map' of the country."

A big tournament seemed like the next logical step for golfers to discover the desert, not just the golfers who were staying for a week or so in one of the local hotels looking for a casual recreational round, but serious golfers, professionals as well as top amateur players.

The $2,000 event at O'Donnell was certainly part of a plan by village officials to bring more visitors to their community. What better way to show that Palm Springs was a destination for golfers than holding a big-money tournament with a great professional field.

And what a professional field it was. In what was billed as the "Greatest Sports Event in Palm Springs History" by organizers, the marquee name in the two-day, seventy-two-hole event was Walter Hagen. In the previous

24

This shot from the San Jacinto Mountains of O'Donnell Golf Club in Palm Springs in the 1980s shows the course almost unchanged from when it first opened in 1927. O'Donnell is the oldest existing course in the Coachella Valley. *Courtesy of Palm Springs Historical Society. All rights reserved.*

two decades, Hagen had almost singlehandedly elevated professional golfers from the ranks of pool hall hustlers to something bordering on respectability. It was still more likely for a top golfer to remain an amateur, like golf's golden boy of the 1920s, Bobby Jones. But Hagen and others were showing that touring the country playing tournaments and exhibitions was a way to make a living.

The PGA (Professional Golfers' Association) of America had existed since 1916, but the touring division of that organization started keeping track of earnings only in 1934. By that time, Hagen had won eleven of what are now recognized as major championships. That included five PGA Championships and four British and U.S. Opens in 1914 and 1919. He had also played on and captained the United States team in the first four biennial Ryder Cup matches between the United States and a team from Great Britain and Ireland starting in 1927. Hagen also lived an unabashed lifestyle. He loved the good things in life, had a flair for the dramatic and reminded fans to stop and smell the roses along the way. Hagen was golf's matinee idol. It was no wonder that Hagen was the liaison between his fellow professionals and the people wanting to bring a tournament to Palm Springs.

For such a major star to come to Palm Springs to play on Thomas O'Donnell's golf course was indeed a coup for the desert. But Hagen was not alone in traveling to the Coachella Valley for the tournament, played on February 12 and 13. Horton Smith, who one year earlier had won the first playing of Bobby Jones's invitational tournament in Augusta, Georgia, which would become known as the Masters, was also in the field. Willie Hunter, Olin Dutra, Ky Laffoon, Leo Diegel, Johnny Revolta, Harry Cooper, Denny Shute, Craig Wood and Henry Picard were other nationally known players in the desert field.

The format was two days of thirty-six holes each over O'Donnell's course. But since the course was only nine holes, that required four loops around the course on February 12 and another four loops on February 13.

When it was over, it was Horton Smith who earned a 1-shot victory over Ky Laffoon. Smith's rounds of 66, 66, 66 and 62 put him at 20-under par to earn $400. Laffoon shot a new eighteen-hole course record of 61 in the final eighteen but missed a birdie putt on the final hole that would have posted a 60 and forced a playoff.

Hagen finished a distant fourteenth at 276, though he handily beat all nine of the amateurs in the event. Sir Walter was certainly the biggest golfing star to have played in the desert to that point.

It was a big moment for the desert to have such world-renowned professionals come to the desert, but it certainly didn't do anything to spur more golf course development. The four courses that had started the golf craze in the desert, the Hotel La Quinta course, the Mashie Course at the Desert Inn, Thomas O'Donnell's golf course and the nine holes at El Mirador Hotel, remained the only significant courses in the area through the 1930s. And when it came to hosting tournaments like the $2,000 event in 1935, the desert was even more limited. The Mashie Course was strictly a short, recreational course. The El Mirador course was struggling with financial problems and was in a windy corridor of the still-barren desert. And the Hotel La Quinta course was quite a bit out of the way for the average golfer without a room reservation at the hotel.

It was the O'Donnell Golf Course, a short but sporty nine-hole layout, that became the location of the desert's most important tournaments in the 1930s and 1940s. These might have started with Hagen's appearance, but it was continued from the 1930s into the 1960s by one of the finest amateur events for men and an equally fine tournament for top female professionals from the West Coast. The Palm Springs Golf Invitational began in 1936, one year after the big professional tournament at O'Donnell's course. Along with the biggest names in amateur golf, the tournament annually featured

Among the famous celebrity golfers and desert residents who frequented O'Donnell Golf Club in Palm Springs in the 1930s and 1940s was famous composer Hoagy Carmichael (far left). Carmichael would later be an early member of Thunderbird Country Club, the desert's first eighteen-hole course. *Photo by Frank S. Partridge. Courtesy of Palm Springs Historical Society. All rights reserved.*

a few of the desert's high-profile celebrities. The 1958 event, for example, included Bob Hope, actor and singer Phil Harris, singer Gordon MacRae and UCLA football coach Red Sanders.

From its debut in 1936 into the 1960s, the tournament also featured one of the most talented amateur golfers from Southern California who would become part of the desert golf landscape: Dr. Frank "Bud" Taylor.

Taylor was a dentist by trade, having earned his degree at the University of Southern California. But if dentistry was his profession, Taylor's love was golf. Like many top players in the 1930s and 1940s, Taylor remained an amateur in the game, much along the lines of the great Bobby Jones.

Taylor certainly ranked among the best amateurs of his time. He won consecutive California Amateur titles in 1954 and 1955. He was a member of three U.S. Walker Cups teams, tied for twenty-ninth in the 1956 U.S.

Open and played in four Masters, a tournament founded by another lifelong amateur, Jones. Taylor was so important to golf in Southern California, both in the Palm Spring area and at his home course of Red Hill in Rancho Cucamonga near his dentistry practice in Pomona, that he was inducted into the Southern California Golf Association's Hall of Fame in 2009

Taylor's impact in the Coachella Valley began in that 1936 Palm Springs Golf Invitational at O'Donnell Golf Course, when he won the inaugural title when he was still just a sixteen-year-old high schooler from Ontario, a little more than an hour to the west of Palm Springs.

As the tournament grew in importance on the West Coast, it attracted the best and the brightest young golfers. But time and again, the best players would have to fight their way past Taylor to win the title. It would take until 1952 for Taylor to win his second title at O'Donnell, but he followed that up with wins in 1955 and 1957. In his last two victories, Taylor finished just ahead of Harvie Ward, the talented amateur from San Francisco who, along with Ken Venturi, made San Francisco the hot spot of amateur golf in the decade. Ward was even the reigning U.S. Amateur champion when he fell just short of Taylor in the 1957 event. But Ward had won the tournament in 1954 and 1956.

Taylor also went on to earn three wins in another of the high-profile amateur events in the desert in the 1950s at Thunderbird Country Club, giving him seven desert titles. But the O'Donnell tournament was in a different class, according to a back-to-back winner in 1958 and 1959.

"I guess I would say that the O'Donnell tournament was one of the best amateur events," said Al Geiberger, who was playing golf at USC when he won the consecutive O'Donnell tournaments, still years away from his PGA Championship win in 1966 or his tour-record round of 59 in 1977. "From the top of the list, well, there was the state amateur. I would say the O'Donnell invitational was right under the state amateur, maybe even better than the Southern California Amateur. And that's because the O'Donnell event had such a great field."

Geiberger, now a longtime desert resident, had never been to the Coachella Valley before being coaxed into entering the O'Donnell event by his USC teammates, who were playing the event as well. For a top college player accustomed to playing courses in the Los Angeles area like Hillcrest, Wilshire and Los Angeles North, O'Donnell was an eye-opening experience.

"I guess the guys on the team had explained it to me," Geiberger said. "We had two sets of tees on every hole, so it was nine holes and we changed tees. It was right up against the mountains. In fact I think we hit over the mountain a couple of times."

Geiberger's 1958 win came over veteran California amateur Bruce McCormick when Geiberger rallied on the last day for a rolled-in 6-under 64 to catch McCormick. Geiberger then rolled in a forty-five-foot birdie putt on the second playoff hole.

Geiberger had made the adjustment to the short O'Donnell course well in part because he knew he was having trouble with his tee shots coming into the tournament.

"I wasn't driving the ball, so I had an old MacGregor 2-wood," he said. "Most players were using the driver, the 3-wood and the 4-wood, but they would take the 2-wood out of the set. But it had a big head, and it worked well as a driver for me. And a lot of the other holes were just layup holes, with a 2-iron or 3-iron off the tee."

The day after his first win in the O'Donnell event, Geiberger saw more of the burgeoning desert golf world.

"Some people took me over and I played Eldorado Country Club," Geiberger said. "I remember reaching up and picking an orange right off of the trees there."

Geiberger's 1959 win wasn't quite as dramatic, as he beat another Southern California amateur, Phil Rogers of La Jolla, by four shots.

"That tournament always had some great players," Geiberger said. "Harvie Ward and Ken Venturi, they were in that group just ahead of me [in stature]. And Gene Littler and Dr. Bud Taylor. That's why I say it might be second to only the state amateur. It really used to be something."

A few years later, Geiberger had turned pro and won another big tournament in the desert, the 1961 Southern California Open at Indian Wells Country Club. He defended that title in 1962 at La Quinta Country Club, where his strongest memories are how far the golf course seemed from civilization and how he 5-putted the first green.

"I loved the desert right away," Geiberger said. "I just loved the feel of it."

While all the top amateurs in the country were coming to the desert for big tournaments, golf course development itself had come to a grinding halt on the Coachella Valley. No significant course had opened in the desert since the El Mirador Hotel course in 1929, though a few small mashie-style courses, a few driving ranges and even a miniature golf course had popped up in the area. The eastern end of the Coachella Valley still had only the nine-hole course at the Hotel La Quinta. But one of the most famous women in the United States was about to change all of that.

Jackie Cochran first tried to make a name for herself selling a line of cosmetics and wigs. But when she took her first trip in an airplane in the early 1930s, Cochran was hooked. Within just a few years, she had earned a commercial pilot's license and was competing in air races. She might not have been as famous as her friend Amelia Earhart, but Cochran was a good enough pilot to set speed records of her own.

She later helped form and promote the Women's Auxiliary Army Corp during World War II and pushed to have female pilots flying noncombat missions during the war. She flew a bomber across the Atlantic Ocean during the war and eventually received the Distinguished Service Medal. It all helped to make her famous, with help from her husband, an industrialist named Floyd Odlum who was at the time one of the richest men in America and who had a majority interests in RKO Studios in Hollywood before selling to Howard Hughes.

Even before the couple was married, Cochran acquired land in Indio, and after their marriage, the couple developed the ranch. By the middle of the 1940s, the couple had decided the Cochran-Odlum Ranch needed at least a few golf holes for visitors and friends to enjoy.

But one of Cochran's friends was not a fan of building just four or five holes. Helen Dettweiler had been a successful amateur golfer before the war, but during the war, she had served in a variety of roles, including in the Women Airforce Service Pilots, or WASP. She was one of the seventeen women chosen to fly B-17 bombers.

Cochran had also been a member of WASP, so the two became friends. When Cochran told Dettweiler of her plans for a handful of holes in the Indio area, Dettweiler said that the course really ought to be a full nine-hole course. Don't do half the job; do the job all the way, the right way. Cochran and Odlum agreed and put Dettweiler in charge of the project. Just as African American Lawrence Crossley had put his stamp on desert golf with his work at the El Mirador golf course in Palm Springs, Helen Dettweiler became one of the first women in the country credited with designing a golf course at the Cochran-Odlum Ranch.

That Dettweiler was able to design a course, oversee its construction and then become the head pro of the course was not a surprise to those who knew her. During the war, before her time in WASP, she had overseen a code-cracking operation for the United States. Before the war, she had done some play-by-play radio work for the Washington Senators baseball team, owned by a golfing buddy of Dettweiler's named Clark Griffith. And while other women remained amateurs in the 1940s and 1950s because there just was no money in women's golf, Dettweiler pushed for the formation of the Women's Professional Golf Association. That association never took off, but Dettweiler was one of the thirteen founding members of the Ladies Professional Golf Association (LPGA) in 1950. And while she would leave Cochran-Odlum Ranch to become a noted teaching pro in the 1950s at other desert courses, her legacy in the desert is as the first woman to design a course in the Coachella Valley.

The Cochran-Odlum Ranch course opened in November 1946, and within a month, the course hosted an exhibition match between the team of Elizabeth Hicks and Dorothy Kielty against the course's head pro, Dettweiler, and another top player who would have long roots in the desert, Beverly Hanson. The course also started hosting women's amateur tournaments in the later 1940s. One of the earliest winners was a fourteen-year-old from Long Beach who would eventually help Dettweiler and others found the LPGA: Marlene Bauer.

"The only thing I remember about the course is there was a little par-3 that ran along north to south along a street," said Marlene Hagge (née Bauer), who is in the LPGA Hall of Fame both as a founder and as a winner of twenty-six tour events. "I won it in 1948, I beat Beverly [Hanson] by like 15 shots. She shot the same score that she had shot the year before winning it, and I beat her by something like 15 shots."

The female players already established in the desert were kind to the Bauer sisters, Marlene remembers.

"Helen Dettweiler was such a nice person, very charming, and a good player," Hagge recalled. "And Beverly Hanson was very nice, and she was a very good player. She belongs in the Hall of Fame, I think, sixteen wins and three majors."

Hagge and her elder sister Alice were fixtures in Southern California women's amateur golf in the 1940s. Marlene would also win the popular Palm Springs Women's Invitational at O'Donnell, the female equivalent of the course's important Palm Springs Golf Invitational for men. That tournament also began in the 1930s and featured not only top amateur players but also celebrity players—or, at least, the wives of famous celebrities.

Tournament golf had become a way of life in the Coachella Valley, whether it was the amateur tournaments at O'Donnell or Cochran-Odlum Ranch or the occasional professional exhibition or tournament played on those courses. But the desert itself, while growing, was still mostly a weekend getaway or vacation area for the rich and famous, with the permanent population still growing slowly. There were those who saw bigger and better things for the desert and its golf scene, though, and those things were just a few years away.

CHAPTER 3
The Golden Era

As golf seasons go, 1942 was a pretty good year for an amateur golfer from Illinois named Johnny Dawson.

Dawson won both the California State Amateur and California State Open titles in 1942, and he added the first of what would eventually be four Southern California Amateur titles. As impressive as all that was, Dawson's gem for the year came in a PGA tournament played at Rancho Santa Fe Country Club in San Diego. The tournament was the Bing Crosby Pro-Am, hosted by the famous crooner and played in Rancho Santa Fe, just outside San Diego, for the last time in 1942 before moving to the Monterey Peninsula of northern California after the war.

With his 1942 win, Dawson became the only amateur golfer to win the Crosby tournament, which would become known as Crosby Clambake. Though it was just a thirty-six-hole event, Dawson's total of 13-under 133 was 3 shots better than Leland Gibson and future U.S. Open champion Lloyd Mangrum. The field also included pretty much every great player of the day, including Ben Hogan, Sam Snead and Byron Nelson. Dawson refused to accept the first-prize check, so Mangrum and Gibson were listed as the co-winners of the professional part of the event.

But 1942 was just a sampling of Dawson's playing career. A top amateur since the 1930s, Dawson had sharpened his playing skills while representing Spalding golf equipment and touring the country playing events while getting other top players to use the Spalding clubs. Dawson played in the first seven Masters tournaments, toured the country playing

Developer and top amateur player Johnny Dawson walks off the first tee at Thunderbird County Club on opening day, January 9, 1951. *Courtesy of Thunderbird Country Club.*

exhibitions with, among others, Gene Sarazen, Walter Hagen and, perhaps the greatest amateur golfer of all time, Bobby Jones. Banned from many United States Golf Association events for years because he had a paid position at Spalding, which caused the governing body of the game to declare him a pro, Dawson eventually was allowed into the USGA's national championships from 1944 on. In 1947, Dawson was second in the U.S. Amateur at the age of forty-four, a staggering achievement. He also played on the 1949 U.S. Walker Cup team.

It was that set of credentials that Dawson brought to a major golf project in the Coachella Valley. The desert had its golf courses, like O'Donnell Golf Course in Palm Springs and Cochran-Odlum Ranch in Indio, but they were nine-hole layouts. There was a growing sense that a real course, an eighteen-hole course, was needed for a desert that was seeing more and more full-time and part-time residents.

Dawson was familiar with the Coachella Valley, having played in the Palm Springs Golf Invitational many times and winning the tournament at

O'Donnell Golf Club in 1940 and 1949. His 140 total score in 1940 was the tournament record.

Dawson was on the lookout for a possible golf development in the desert, something along the lines of what he had developed in 1947 at Mission Valley Country Club in San Diego. What Dawson eventually found was a struggling dude ranch about ten miles east of the village of Palm Springs called Thunderbird. It was there that Dawson, a team of desert investors and designers and pros hand-selected by Dawson put together the desert's first eighteen-hole golf course surrounded by home lots.

It was a simple idea that actually became the blueprint that changed the Coachella Valley from a quiet, serene desert into what locals would called the Winter Golf Capital of the World in less than a decade. The group that Dawson brought together to build and manage the club, to be called Thunderbird Country Club, would, in fact, be the key personalities in an explosion of golf courses in the desert. Course names that would become familiar across the country—Thunderbird, Tamarisk, Indian Wells, Bermuda Dunes, Eldorado and La Quinta Country Clubs—would all be built in the 1950s, and all would be touched in some way by the original Thunderbird group.

Dawson was joined in the Thunderbird project by Barney Hinkle, Tony Burke and Frank Bogert, all local businessmen and promoters of the desert. Bogert, at one time the publicist for the Racquet Club in Palm Springs and El Mirador Hotel, would eventually go on to become the unofficial mayor of Palm Springs and then the official elected mayor of the town. A statue of Bogert on a horse stands outside Palm Springs City Hall and confirms his status as the "Cowboy Mayor." But in the late 1940s, Bogert was the manager and part owner of the dude ranch trying to figure out what to do with the Thunderbird land. A golf course seemed to be the answer, since the desert's existing golf courses were growing in popularity. Many of the celebrities who had vacationed at places like El Mirador, La Quinta Hotel and the Desert Inn were now starting to buy property in the Coachella Valley. Bob and Dolores Hope bought two homes in Palm Springs in the 1940s, and others, such as singer Al Jolson, were having homes built.

Since many of the desert's visitors—celebrities, corporate executives or just the well-heeled—played golf on their trips to the area, why not build an eighteen-hole course and attract visitors to buy property and join the private Thunderbird Country Club?

In finding a head pro of his club, Dawson reached out to Jimmy Hines. Hines was a good enough player to have won nine PGA Tour

Before Thunderbird Country Club was a golf course, it was a dude ranch. Here, in 1947, are Thunderbird Ranch founder Frank Bogert, actress Babbs Meel and Palm Springs realtor Barney Hinkel on the set of the Warner Brothers motion picture *Two Guys from Texas*. *Courtesy of Thunderbird Country Club.*

events between 1933 and 1945, reached the semifinals of three PGA Championships and the quarterfinals three other times and played in the first ten Masters. Hines was the head pro at North Shore Country Club in Chicago when Dawson asked him to be the head pro at Thunderbird in the winters. Hines came to the desert and brought some of his members to the new course as well. Hines also brought along his assistant pro, Eddie Susalla.

Jimmy Hines (right) was the first head professional at Thunderbird Country Club and was later an official at Eldorado Country Club. Hines is seen here with a young aspiring pro from San Diego, future U.S. Open champion Gene Littler. *Courtesy of Thunderbird Country Club.*

Dawson might have been a golfer, but he also had key connections that helped the Thunderbird real estate venture. Dawson's home course was Lakeside Country Club in Burbank, one of a handful of courses in the Los Angeles area that was populated by some of the biggest names in the entertainment business. Lakeside members included Bob Hope, Bing Crosby (a five-time Lakeside club champion), Ronald Reagan, W.C. Fields, Gene Autry and others.

Eddie Susalla (left) with Thunderbird Country Club member Desi Arnaz. Susalla, an assistant pro at Thunderbird and later head pro at Indian Wells Country Club, is credited with inventing the golf cart to help older members at Thunderbird continue playing as they aged. *Photo by Gail Thompson/Gayle's Studio Collection, courtesy of Tracy Conrad. Courtesy of Palm Springs Historical Society. All rights reserved.*

Dawson could easily pitch his new project in the Coachella Valley to stars who loved golf and already knew what the desert offered in terms of weather and peace and quiet away from the bustle of Hollywood.

Dawson selected architect Lawrence Hughes to design a course along the dunes of the desert and the grounds of the dude ranch. Hughes had learned some of the golf course design business as a construction supervisor for none other than Donald Ross, the famous Scottish designer whose courses included Pinehurst No. 2 in North Carolina and East Lake Golf Club in Atlanta. Hughes had been Dawson's choice as architect when Dawson built Mission Valley Country Club in San Diego. Just three years later, Dawson reached out for Hughes again, this time to produce in the desert a golf course that could at once challenge golfers and allow them to play at or close to the handicaps they held in the summer at their home courses in the Midwest or Pacific Northwest.

The project, complete with golf course, was announced in March 1950, with hopes that the course would be open by the start of 1951. With Dawson as president, Thunderbird Country Club opened on January 9, 1951. Hughes hit the first shot, Dawson shot a course-record 2-under 70 and the Coachella Valley would never been the same again. Among the

The key group that put Thunderbird Country Club into place. *From left*: clubhouse architect William F. Cody, early investor William Jason, founder Frank Bogert, golf course architect Lawrence Hughes, course developer and founder Johnny Dawson, realtor Barney Hinkle, early investor Paul Browne and Coachella Valley publicist Anthony Burke. *Courtesy of Thunderbird Country Club.*

membership when the course opened—or, at least, in the first few months of the course's opening—were original investors Bob Hope; baseball star Ralph Kiner and his wife, tennis star Nancy Chaffee; Desi Arnaz and Lucille Ball; and Bing Crosby.

Thunderbird would continue to grow in popularity and national recognition. The celebrities helped draw the spotlight to the course, but it was more than just the Hollywood crowd that was drawn to the desert for golf. Captains of American industry were also coming to the desert for the weather and the golf. One such person was Ernest Beech, who was the president of the Ford Motor Company. He was so taken by his desert getaway that when Ford began production of a new car in 1954 for the 1955 model year, Beech convinced his company to call the new car the Thunderbird. Late in 1954, the first Ford Thunderbird was presented to Johnny Dawson and his wife, Velma, who, as a puppeteer, had created the Howdy Dowdy marionette. The photograph of the Dawsons and their new Thunderbird still is proudly displayed in the Thunderbird Country Club clubhouse.

As was all too common in the era, country clubs tended to be separated into Jewish and non-Jewish clubs. In the Coachella Valley, that meant a Jewish country club would naturally follow the opening of Thunderbird. That was particularly true with so many Jewish stars from entertainment calling the desert a part-time home. So just about one year after Thunderbird opened, in February 1952, a new club called Tamarisk Country Club opened just a few miles away. The club included residential lots called the Colony. Designed by William P. Bell, the course was similar to Thunderbird in that it was laid out along the natural dunes and flat desert landscape. The idea of bulldozers molding the desert in dramatic designs was still years away.

Among the charter members of the club were Jewish stars like Danny Kaye and the Marx Brothers but also Bob Hope, actor Gordon MacRae and even actor George Montgomery and his wife, singer Dinah Shore, who was still years away from making her own huge imprint on golf in the Coachella Valley. Still, it was known that the Jewish members at Tamarisk would not be playing at Thunderbird, except, of course, for the occasional high-profile pro-am.

While the star-studded membership of Tamarisk was great for the desert, the true news was who the club managed to snare as the golf professional. Ben Hogan had won both the U.S. Open and Masters in 1950 and certainly seemed to be regaining his status as the game's greatest player after the

Ben Hogan might have been the most famous golfer in the world when he settled in to the Coachella Valley, becoming the head professional at Tamarisk Country Club in 1952. The desert's warm winter weather was good for Hogan's leg that had been badly damaged in a 1949 car accident. *Courtesy of Thunderbird Country Club.*

horrible 1949 head-on bus accident that left his body mangled and broken. But in an era when even the top players in the game took winter jobs as golf professionals at clubs, Hogan was a prize catch. He was persuaded to become the head pro at Tamarisk, though ironically Hogan had told his friend Johnny Dawson just a few years earlier that golf in the middle of the desert would never work, or so Dawson loved to say. Now Hogan was the pro at the desert's second eighteen-hole course for what was rumored to be a salary of $90,000. In announcing the hiring, club officials said Hogan's hiring was "in line with [the] overall program of making Tamarisk one of the best courses in the country."

Hogan certainly enjoyed the desert, and it didn't hurt that the warm desert winters allowed him to play golf and practice as he tried to regain strength in his badly damaged legs. And he had good friends in the area, like Dawson and Bob and Dolores Hope. He even gave lessons to Dolores Hope, who would laugh years later, saying that Hogan was a nice man and a great teacher, far from the icy, menacing image of Hogan the player.

America grew to love Lucille Ball and her husband, Desi Arnaz, among the earliest members at Thunderbird Country Club, seen here opening the door to their home. *Courtesy of Thunderbird Country Club.*

With Hogan on board and well-known members, the desert had another high-profile country club to attract new residents and tourists.

Hogan was an important part of Tamarisk at first, but he left the club after just a few years to concentrate on his touring life. Hogan was followed as head pro at Tamarisk by another legend, though Ellsworth Vines's legend had been built in tennis. In the 1930s, there was no better male tennis player in the world than Vines. Four times, he finished a season as the number-one player in the world; he won two U.S. Open titles and one Wimbledon title, losing in the finals at Wimbledon another time. After turning pro, he won five professional Slam titles. No less than tennis legend Don Budge said Vines was the best player in the world.

But bored with the game and unsure where tennis was heading, Vines simply walked away from the court at the age of twenty-eight and focused on golf. And he was good, perhaps not as good as he was in tennis, but good. He never won on the PGA Tour, but he did win three smaller tournaments and posted forty-seven top-ten finishes in tour events. In 1951, three years before taking the Tamarisk job, Vines lost to Walter Burkemo on the first extra hole of a semifinal match in the PGA Championship.

Vines and his younger brother, Ed, would be instrumental in other courses in the desert like Bermuda Dunes and La Quinta Country Clubs, and the tennis-legend-turned-golfer would stay in the desert the rest of his life.

The promise of Tamarisk as a top club caused M.O. Anderson, the president of Tamarisk, to give one of the all-time great understatements on the future of golf in the Coachella Valley.

"Palm Springs can be the golf capital of the world," Anderson said. "So many good golfers enjoy playing in the winter, before two years are over, we'll need another 18-hole golf course."

Anderson couldn't have known that half a dozen important courses would be open in the desert by the end of the decade. The next course in that line would rely heavily on the roots established at Thunderbird.

Milt Hicks was a member of one of the most important families of early Palm Springs. His father, Alva, was an important figure in the incorporation of Palm Springs in 1938 and was also one of the city's first city councilmen. The Hicks family was key to bringing water to Palm Springs through the Palm Springs Mutual Water Agency, digging a canal that ran fourteen miles from the Whitewater Canyon to Palm Springs before people knew there was plenty of water under their feet in the desert's aquifer. Milt Hicks later took over the family hardware business in Palm Springs.

Hicks also loved his golf so much that, by the end of the 1950s, he was known as Mr. Golf in the desert. He was an early member at Thunderbird in 1951 and five years later helped create another famous course in the desert, Indian Wells Country Club. Hicks was one of the original six investors in the new club, along with Thunderbird members Desi Arnaz, Phil Harris and Paul Prom. Just as Hogan had told Johnny Dawson that golf in the desert would never work, Harris had famously told people that the courses in the middle of the valley ten miles or more from the center of Palm Springs were so far out that "even the Indians won't be able to find them." Now he was an investor.

Among the earliest trendsetters and most important figures in golf in the Coachella Valley in the 1950s were J.E. "Dad" French (left) of O'Donnell Golf Club and Milt Hicks of Thunderbird Country Club and later Indian Wells Country Club. *Courtesy of Thunderbird Country Club.*

When looking for someone to design the course and serve as club manager, the developers called on Eddie Susalla, who had been the assistant pro at Thunderbird to Jimmy Hines. Nine holes opened in 1956 and another nine holes in 1957 at a reported cost of $75,000. At the corner of the development, Arnaz would open the Indian Wells Hotel.

In his time at Thunderbird, Susalla had been credited with inventing what is today a golf essential, the golf cart. As the story goes, Susalla had seen a

Many places may claim to be the birthplace of the golf cart, but Thunderbird Country Club makes a strong claim with assistant pro Eddie Susalla as inventor. Here, the course's grounds staff line up the carts at the course. *Courtesy of Thunderbird Country Club.*

handicapped man using a powered vehicle to get around sidewalks and cross streets. With several members of Thunderbird getting older and having trouble walking eighteen holes, Susalla decided to get a powered cart and add metal holding areas on either side so that the cart could hold a golf bag. Eventually carts became so popular at Thunderbird that walking players were required to give way to the motorized players.

A year later, another course would open in Indian Wells, an area named after an old water well dug by Cahulla Indians years earlier. This time, it was Jimmy Hines who started the process, identifying a 792-acre fruit farm for sale tucked against the base of the Santa Rosa Mountains. Hines would then ask Johnny Dawson to come on board the project, which was originally announced as a thirty-six-hole project. That was eventually scaled back to an eighteen-hole layout called Eldorado Country Club and designed by, not surprisingly, Lawrence Hughes. The original investment group included Robert McCullough, who, among other things, had built airplane engines and car superchargers before going into business making chainsaws. By 1958, McCullough had bought out the other investors and owned the club and all of the land himself.

As had been true at Thunderbird, Tamarisk and Indian Wells, the cross-pollination of memberships continued at Eldorado. The first men's club champion at the course was Bing Crosby, who also won a club championship at Thunderbird. Other Eldorado members included Gordon MacRae, actor Randolph Scott, radio star Freeman Gosden and various corporate leaders from across the country.

The next great desert course of the 1950s was opened in March 1959 by two of the desert's most colorful figures, Ray Ryan and Ernie Dunlevie.

Dunlevie's life reads like something out of a novel, a Walter Mitty character come to life. Dunlevie and his mother had driven across the country from New Jersey to the Coachella Valley in the 1930s for a vacation and simply never went back. It was the start of a life that pretty much any man would envy.

A notoriously private man, Dunlevie would at times let a story of his past slip out—like his time in World War II flying bombing missions out of China in a B-29. You would have to learn from other people the story of how Dunlevie was shot down over Burma and forced to parachute out of the plane at eighteen thousand feet. The crew somehow reunited on the ground, and after a few weeks, Dunlevie and his crew were rescued, with just one crew member losing his life in the incident. Dunlevie was awarded the Distinguished Flying Cross and the Air Medal with Oak Leaf Cluster, not that he would tell you that.

That close-to-the-vest approach made Dunlevie a trusted real estate agent in the desert, and his reputation spread as one who would keep his clients' lives confidential. Of course, his clients were people like actors Cary Grant and Fernando Llamas. He became such a close friend to Clark Gable that Dunlevie served as a pallbearer at Gable's funeral. Dunlevie liked to tell the story of how one of his clients, Howard Hughes, would call in the middle of the night to announce he was coming to pick up Dunlevie. Ernie would get in the back seat of the car with Hughes, and they would be driven around the desert by a chauffeur, with Ernie and Howard just talking business. Then Hughes would drop Dunlevie back at his home a few hours later.

In golf, Dunlevie is one of the two people—Milt Hicks is the other—credited with talking Bob Hope into putting Hope's name on the desert PGA Tour event. He was friends with both Dwight Eisenhower and Gerald Ford. And after they met in 1960, Dunlevie became Arnold Palmer's perhaps best friend in the desert.

Dunlevie and his partner, Terry Ray, bought some farmland in the natural dunes of the desert away from the mountains, with a plan for a residential golf course. At some point, Dunlevie bought out Ray's half and then sold that half to Ray Ryan. Ryan made his money as an oil wildcatter. He had bought El Mirador Hotel after World War II when the U.S. Army no longer needed it as a hospital. With Ryan leading an investment group he eventually

PGA West. *Courtesy of Graeme Baxter Golf Art.*

bought out, El Mirador had once again become a destination resort for Hollywood's elite. Ryan had formed friendships with El Mirador guests like William Holden and Fernando Llamas. Ryan and Holden eventually formed the Mount Kenya Club in Africa. Ryan did have at least two bad habits. He gambled a lot and tended to hang around too often with known mobsters.

The Dunlevie-Ryan partnership opened Bermuda Dunes Country Club in March 1959, a wide and challenging course designed by William P. Bell, the same designer who had done Tamarisk Country Club seven years earlier. With the combined celebrity connections of Dunlevie and Ryan, Bermuda Dunes could challenge pretty much any desert club in star power, with names like Gable, Holden and Llamas as members.

While other golf courses were beginning to be developed in the desert, including one in Palm Springs that the city would eventually buy and turn into its municipal course, one last great name in the area would open before the end of the decade. It would be at the east end of the desert with a course across the street from La Quinta Hotel. It was named La Quinta Country Club. Three men, Leonard Ettleson, Roy Crummer and John Elsbach, had bought La Quinta Hotel and some land just to the east of it. They decided they could build a country club on 130 acres and then use the course as both a private club as well as a course for the guests at the hotel. The nine-hole course at the hotel built in 1927 had been allowed to be consumed by the desert after World War II and was now being used to grow date palms and alfalfa.

In one last connection to the courses that started the golden era of golf development in the 1950s, Lawrence Hughes was selected to design La Quinta Country Club. The course opened in November 1959, a fitting end to what had been a remarkable decade of growth fueled by men with huge dreams and huge personalities. The title of Winter Golf Capital of the World, pushed hard by the local *Desert Sun* newspaper and other marketers of the desert, didn't seem like a stretch. The desert and golf had been married in the 1950s. But it was an explosion of golf events there that secured the desert's image as a golf mecca.

CHAPTER 4
For Money and Country

As recreational golf grew in the desert in the 1950s, one thing seemed evident. The area needed a professional golf tournament of its own. Not just one-day exhibitions or two-day events or team competitions, but an honest-to-goodness professional tournament.

Since Thunderbird Country Club was the first eighteen-hole course in the desert in 1951, and with top-caliber players like Johnny Dawson and Jimmy Hines in key roles at the club, Thunderbird was a logical site for a big event. Helping matters was the fact that so many of the top celebrities who were calling Thunderbird home were friends with many of the professional players of the day. Seriously, which pros didn't already know Bob Hope and Bing Crosby? An invitational pro-am seemed a natural.

The first Thunderbird Pro-Member Open was held in January 1952, just one year after the course opened. As strange as it sounds, the professional portion of the tournament seemed to be an afterthought to the pro-am division. Jim Ferrier and Dr. Cary Middlecoff tied for first in the pro division of the event at 10-under 134, besting a field that included no less than Byron Nelson, Ben Hogan, Jimmy Demaret and Julius Boros, to name just a few.

But most of the headlines went to professional Dutch Harrison, who won the pro-am division with his playing partners Paul Prom, Grant Withers and Paris Letsinger. The Thunderbird members were as big an attraction for the event as the pros, and those same members were serious about winning the pro-am title. And perhaps just a few of them were also interested in how their Calcutta bets were doing.

NO.	PLAYER	HDCP	TKT. NO.	TICKET HOLDER	SOLD FOR	BUYER	TOTAL POOL
							11,200
1	Bruce McCormick -1		6367	H+M	2900°°	Jim Hamm	12,940
2	Jim Ferrie -1		3875	H.Maris	2700°°	A.A.Littler	14,560
3	M.Hicks-5-R.Roos-1-R.Whaley-2		1955	J.Allgair	1200°°	E.Stainton	15,280
4	F.Hoover-1-M.Ferentz-2		2745	W.P.Millner	1500°°	C.Anderson	16,180
5	B.McKinney-2 & Troyer 2-GO...-BMChase2		2713	417	1400°°	B.Gengenbach	17,020
6	Field #1		3389	Mac	1700°°	Ross Clare	18,040
7	Jennings 0-J.Ecklund 2-A.Todd 2		1513	G.Thomas	1900°°	C.Anderson	19,180
8	Dwyer 3-B.Higgins 5-D.Meyers 3		2675	3 Jokers	1200°°	J.O.Lynch	19,900
9	Stanley 0-		2599	M.O.Anderson	3000°°	Mrs J.R.Clare	20,680
10	Pennel 1-B.Henneken 1		2274		1100°°	T.Torrence	21,340
11	J.Earle 4-C.Hammond 4-BMCrary4-J.Anderson	11,265	C.Needham		600°°	B.Gengenbach	21,700
12	Burge 4-H.Miller 5-F.Hixon 2		1753	T.Torrence	950°°	M.Hicks	22,270
13	J.Lovegren-0		3560	R.D.	2100°°	C.Needham	23,530
14	Field #2		2344		2000°°	F.Whitman	24,730
15	Fahy 4-G.McRae 4-B.Leonard4-J.Wilson 4		6275	H+M	1000°°	Mrs.Leonard	25,350
16	Gene Littler 0		1508	Harry+Lewis	3800°°	J.Rector	27,610
17	Bill Callister4-J.Harelson4-J.Evans4-J.McPherton	1675	H+M		2200°°	B.Taylor	28,950
18	Tommy Jacobs-2-H.Borkman 3		10852	A.Green	2100°°	Mrs.Stainton	30,190
19	Field #3		3300	P.Singer	1600°°	R.Singer	31,150
20	Bud Taylor 0		6530	P.Vesom	3600°°	P.Singer	33,310
21	Cooper 2-J.Cunacov 2		8830	H.Reichel	1400°°	C.Anderson	34,150
22	Fletcher Jones-0		7080	J.DeBruleski	1300°°	J.Rector	34,950
23	Bobby Gardner-0		4152	J.Koener	2500°°	C.Needham	36,430
24	Field #4		11,285		2200°°	Mrs.Manning	37,750
25	Johnny Dawson-0		6394	H+M	4600°°	M.Eaton	40,510

One activity that helped make the Thunderbird Invitational professional tournament so popular was a spirited Calcutta gambling pool. Note the $40,510 total betting pool for a tournament that offered no more than a $15,000 purse for the pros. *Courtesy of Thunderbird Country Club.*

Calcuttas were a common practice in golf up until the 1950s. Basically, a Calcutta is an auction-style draft. People—in this case the members at Thunderbird—would bid on the professional players they thought would win the tournament, or maybe they would bet on the celebrity amateurs who were in the field. The bidding would become fierce, and with the well-heeled membership at Thunderbird, the prices would go higher and higher. It was not uncommon for the Calcutta pool at the Thunderbird event to be several times higher than the professional division purse, which in 1952 was just $5,000.

Problems came later in the 1950s when fraud in Calcutta events started to become rampant at country clubs across the country. Amateurs would lie about their handicaps and sandbag their way to victory and big money. There was even talk that some pros were being paid off to potentially throw a round or fake an injury or illness, just to ensure that some big-money bettors would see that the players they were backing would win the event.

Things became so bad that, in 1955, Richard Tufts, the president of the United States Golf Association, issued a position paper for the USGA stating that "the United States Golf Association urges its Member Clubs, all golf associations and all other sponsors of golf competitions to prohibit gambling in connection with tournaments. This refers to all forms of gambling, including Calcutta auction pools, pari-mutuel betting, lotteries and other devices."

While the Calcutta might have been fading in acceptance a bit, the Thunderbird tournament continued as a popular event. Professionals were playing events at other desert clubs throughout the 1950s, but the Thunderbird tournament began offering something the other events couldn't: official status for the touring division of the PGA of America, the forerunner of the PGA Tour. Check the PGA Tour record of Jimmy Demaret, a three-time winner of the Masters, and you won't see any mention of his win at the 1953 Thunderbird Invitational. That's because the first two events in 1952 and

Jimmy Demaret was a top player of his time, winning three Masters and three Thunderbird Invitationals in the desert. He also lost a playoff in the 1964 Palm Springs Invitational. *Courtesy of La Quinta Historical Society.*

1953 were not official money events. But that changed for the 1954 event, and winner Fred Haas earned not only an official PGA Tour win but also money toward the tour's money list.

The tournament continued to grow, with Shelly Mayfield winning in 1955 and Demaret coming back in 1956 and 1957 for victories, meaning he had three wins in the six events.

The 1958 Thunderbird event produced a popular local winner, even though that winner was best known as a San Francisco star. Ken Venturi was one of the finest amateurs the game had in the 1950s, as was his running mate from the Bay Area, Harvie Ward. Both were protégés of Eddie Lowrey, a millionaire car dealer from San Francisco who was best known in golf for being the ten-year-old caddie for Francis Ouimet when Ouimet won the 1913 U.S. Open at the Country Club in Brookline, Massachusetts.

Lowrey remained involved in golf all his life, eventually serving on the executive board of the United States Golf Association. Lowrey was one of the men behind a famous four-ball match between his players, Venturi and Ward, against Byron Nelson and Ben Hogan in 1956, a competition recounted in Mark Frost's book *The Match*.

At one point, Lowrey asked his friend Byron Nelson to take a look at Venturi's swing and help out the budding star. Nelson decided to rebuild Venturi's swing, and Lowrey set it up for Nelson and Venturi to spend time at Thunderbird, where Lowrey was a member, as was his longtime friend Bob Hope. From then on, Venturi had a connection with Thunderbird that lasted throughout his life.

Venturi won the tournament in 1958 and the $1,500 first prize and a new Ford Thunderbird. But if you had any questions about the Calcutta and whether it had disappeared, think about this story from Venturi's autobiography. It was customary for whoever had money on a player in a Calcutta to share part of the winnings with the player. Venturi said he received an envelope from the man who had bid $200 to take Venturi that week. When Venturi opened the envelope later, it contained ten $1,000 bills.

The next year, Venturi tried to defend his title at the Thunderbird Invitational, and Demaret was in position for a fourth win in the tournament. But both players could do no better than finish tied for second. Posting a blistering 10-under 62 in the final round to erase a 5-shot deficit at the start of the day was the reigning Masters champion and 1958 money leader for the tour, Arnold Palmer. It was Palmer's first win in the desert. It would not be his last.

The Thunderbird Invitational certainly gave the desert a significant place on the professional tour, but to get international recognition, the Coachella

Robert Hudson of Portland, Oregon, a member at Thunderbird Country Club, chats with Lord Brabazon of Tara, who was captain of the Royal and Ancient Golf Club of St. Andres in 1952 and 1953. It was Hudson who paid for most of the expenses to have the Ryder Cup played at Thunderbird Country Club in 1955 and Eldorado Country Club in 1959. *Courtesy of Thunderbird Country Club.*

Valley took advantage of a biennial event that was frankly lagging in interest. The Ryder Cup came to the Coachella Valley for the same reason the Ryder Cup existed at all in the 1950s, Robert Hudson. Hudson was a grocer and a produce distributor from Portland, Oregon, and a lover of the game of golf. While Hudson was said to never be better than a double-digit handicapper, his love of the game and his wealth helped save the Ryder Cup from the scrap heap in 1947.

The biennial matches between the United States and a team from Great Britain and Ireland had started in 1927. But after the 1937 matches, the competition was suspended from 1939 through 1945 due to the ravages of World War II. Hudson, or at least his money, almost singlehandedly saved the matches from extinction. First, Hudson convinced his home course of Portland Country Club to host the matches. Then Hudson, a friend of the president of the British PGA, Lord Brabazon of Tara, paid out of his own pocket for the Great Britain and Ireland team to sail to New York on the *Queen Mary* and then get the team to Portland by train. Without Hudson, the 1947 matches might not have been played, and there is a serious chance the matches might not have ever started up again.

While Hudson was from Portland, he was also one of the first of a rare bird known in the Coachella Valley as the snowbird. Simply put, a snowbird is someone who flees the winter cold and snow and rain of areas like the Pacific Northwest or the upper Midwest or Canada to spend long amounts of time in the Southwest or Florida. Not surprisingly, one of the appeals of the Coachella Valley for snowbirds is golf.

This was also true in the 1950s, as Hudson demonstrated. By 1955, Hudson had become a powerful member of the PGA of America's advisory board. He was also a member at Thunderbird Country Club, which had opened in 1951. Hudson's influence and money, along with the expertise of Johnny Dawson and Jimmy Hines, helped award Thunderbird the Ryder Cup in 1955, a stunning coup for the young club even if the matches were still fighting to recover from the long layoff during the war. And when the matches went over budget, it was Hudson who stepped in to make up the difference. As the 1955 Ryder Cup approached, the matches were starting to regain some international interest, and the 1955 cup certainly captured the attention of the desert.

Part of that budget went toward putting the Thunderbird course, very friendly for members, into the kind of shape that could challenge the best players in the world. That included stretching the course out to 6,600 yards, about 300 yards longer than Lawrence Hughes's original design. In a story in the local paper, changes were said to include "new traps to require accurate second shots, and new rough to catch wayward drives." And the course had to accommodate more people than it was accustomed to, so some cart paths were added and widened. The extra space was needed, since more than three thousand fans were reported to be on the course for the matches.

As one might expect with so many entertainment stars in the Thunderbird membership, the matches featured their fair share of Hollywood star power. The pro-am early in the week included some of Thunderbird's famous celebrity members, such as Bob Hope and Bing Crosby.

When it came time for the actual matches, it was a familiar Ryder Cup story. The Americans had won the four Ryder Cups played since the end of World War II and the two played just before the war. The 1955 matches would extend that winning streak to seven straight for the U.S. team. Led by

U.S. captain Chick Harbert (left) and Great Britain and Ireland captain Dai Rees hold the Ryder Cup while cup matches benefactor Robert Hudson smiles before the 1955 matches at Thunderbird Country Club. *Courtesy of Thunderbird Country Club.*

players like Sam Snead, Doug Ford, Jerry Barber and Cary Middlecoff, the Americans won the foursome matches, or alternate-shot matches, three to one. In the next day's singles matches, the Americans padded their lead with five points in eight matches for an overall victory of eight to four. For those who cared to pay attention, and that might have been true more of people in Great Britain than in the United States, the 1955 Ryder Cup stamped the desert as a world-class golf destination, not just a local getaway for Hollywood stars. No less an authority than British golf commentator Henry

Longhurst said he thought the bar at Thunderbird was the best in the world because it provided a perfect view of the golf course. Such comments were read throughout the United Kingdom, giving Thunderbird and the desert some needed international public relations.

The power and the purse strings of Robert Hudson and the knowledge of Dawson and Hines came into play again four years later to get the desert a second Ryder Cup. If Thunderbird hosting the matches in 1955, just four years after the course opened, was a surprise, it was perhaps more of a surprise that Eldorado Country Club, just a few miles east of Thunderbird, played host to the 1959 matches just two years after that layout opened.

As was true at Portland Country Club in 1947 and Thunderbird Country Club in 1955, it was Hudson who footed much of the bill to ensure that the matches went on at Eldorado. Hudson, who was a member at Eldorado as well as Thunderbird, paid transportation costs for the matches and for a lavish welcoming dinner for the Great Britain and Ireland (GB&I) team. Hudson truly could be called the man who saved the Ryder Cup by this time.

If there was a difference in these matches, it was that the Ryder Cup belonged to the GB&I team after a surprising seven and a half to four and a half win in the 1957 matches at Lindrick Golf Club in Rotherhan, England. It was the first American loss in the matches since 1933. The U.S. team was out to regain the cup and to ensure that the GB&I team didn't record its first-ever win on U.S. soil.

Much like the 1955 matches, the 1959 matches were a colorful and celebrity-filled affair. Bob Hope was the honorary captain of the U.S. team while, once again, Lord Brabazon of Tara was the GB&I honorary captain. A pro-member tournament featured the Ryder Cup players and other pros paired with Eldorado members. One of the pros playing in the pro-member but not on the Ryder Cup team that year was Arnold Palmer. Later in the week came the celebrity event with players like Hope and Crosby and celebrity desert golfers like actors Randolph Scott and James Garner side-by-side with the Ryder Cup players

The real excitement of the matches came well before the first ball was struck. After arriving in Los Angeles, the GB&I team boarded a small commuter plane, the kind that was becoming more and more popular between Los Angeles and the desert. But during the stormy flight, the plane suddenly dropped from about thirteen thousand feet to about nine thousand feet. Eventually, the pilots were able to stabilize the plane and turned back to Los Angeles for a safe landing. Hudson arranged for another flight, but GB&I captain Dai Rees, faced with a shaken team, decided it was better to charter a bus for the long drive from Los Angeles to the Coachella Valley.

Sam Snead
teeing off in the
1959 Ryder Cup
with teammate
Cary Middlecoff
watching in the
background
and the iconic
Eldorado Country
Club clubhouse in
the background.
*Courtesy of Desert
Classic Archives.*

About the only changes Eldorado staff made to the golf course for the
matches was swapping the ninth and eighteenth holes for the two-day affair.
But it would take more than a change in course routing to help the defenders

hold on to the cup. The Americans boasted a powerful team that included Sam Snead as the playing captain leading a squad with Bob Rosburg, Julius Boros, Art Wall, Mike Souchak, Dow Finsterwald, Doug Ford and Cary Middlecoff. There was no way this team was going to lose, though the Great Britain and Ireland team managed to trail by just a point, two and a half to one and a half, after the four opening foursome matches. But when the eight singles matches were played, the American strength was overwhelming. The Americans won five matches outright, with Wall's match against Christy O'Connor ending seven and six on the twelfth green. Snead and Rosburg won by identical six and five scores, meaning they didn't see the fourteenth on that day. Two other matches were halved, giving a half point to each player, and GB&I managed just one victory, from Eric Brown over Cary Middlecoff. The Americans won singles six to two and the overall matched eight and a half to three and a half, a drubbing by any account.

That would have seemed to be the end of the desert's Ryder Cup story, as the matches began to grow in popularity and courses in the East and Midwest began hosting the biennial affair. But there was one more flirtation between the Ryder Cup and the desert. That came with the matches that were awarded to the TPC Stadium Course at PGA West in La Quinta for 1991. The Stadium Course, a beast of a layout designed by Pete Dye, had opened in late 1985 but already had a growing reputation as perhaps the toughest golf course in the country. The developer of the course was Landmark Land Company, and two principals of the company, Ernie Vossler and Joe Walser, had deep roots in the PGA of America. So the Ryder Cup would come to the Coachella Valley for a third time. It was a huge coup for Landmark, Vossler, Walser and the desert. The Ryder Cup had become a spirited, even contentious competition with worldwide attention, as the GB&I team had become a full European team that was beating the Americans in the 1980s. Just as the 1955 matches at Thunderbird had brought publicity to the desert, the 1991 matches would do the same by being beamed around the world from La Quinta desert.

Only it never happened. In addition to PGA West, Landmark was building other courses across the country, and one, the Ocean Course at Kiawah Island in South Carolina, was another Pete Dye beauty. Somehow an agreement was reached to move the matches away from PGA West and to Kiawah Island. Those 1991 matches turned into the most memorable matches in the history of the cup, the fabled War by the Shore that came down to the last putt in the last match as the Americans earned a hard-fought and perhaps contentious win over the surging European team.

Above: A made-for-television event featuring four winners of important tournaments in 1961 was taped at La Quinta Country Club in early 1962. The participants were, from left, Jerry Barber, 1961 PGA Championship winner; Jack Nicklaus, 1961 U.S. Amateur winner; television host Jimmy Demaret; 1961 Masters winner, Gary Player; and 1961 U.S. Open winner, Gene Littler. *Courtesy of La Quinta Historical Society.*

Opposite: Pete Dye's dramatic golf course designs helped to reshape the desert landscape. *Courtesy of La Quinta Historical Society.*

In November 1963, La Quinta Country Club and the Coachella Valley were broadcast to the nation through the CBS Match-Play Classic. Promoting the matches here are, *from left to right*, Leonard Ettelson, an original owner of the club; Ed Crowley, a founding member of the club; golf pro Tommy Armour; and famed tennis star and desert golf pro Ellsworth Vines. *Courtesy of La Quinta Historical Society.*

The late 1950s and the early 1960s featured plenty of golf on television in the form of taped competitions between two or perhaps three or four players. La Quinta Country Club seemed to become the home of such events more than other clubs in the desert, though taped events were also played at O'Donnell Golf Course. One of the most interesting of the La Quinta matches was taped in January 1962 between the winners of the four major championships based in the United States in 1961. That field included U.S. Open winner Gene Littler, Masters winner Gary Player, PGA Championship winner Jerry Barber and the two-time U.S. Amateur winner from Ohio, Jack Nicklaus. Nicklaus had just turned pro and was being thrown in against some of the biggest names in the game for the event. Littler won the event, but Nicklaus and La Quinta received some nice television exposure.

La Quinta Country Club also hosted a big television event in 1963, the $166,000 CBS Match-Play Classic, a team match-play event taped in November 1963. Sixteen teams were in the event, and matches were taped and shown one at a time as the bracket progressed. The players stayed at La Quinta Hotel during the week, as did the CBS crew. The tournament was such a success for the folks at La Quinta Country Club, who were struggling for membership at the time, that they invited CBS back to do the whole thing over again in 1964.

In just a decade, the Coachella Valley had gone from an area with few golf courses and tournaments dominated by amateurs to a place known for national and international professional events televised across the country. But the best for the desert—the pros and television—was yet to come.

CHAPTER 5
Arnie, Bob and the 1960s

Arnold Palmer peered through the fence at a finely manicured golf course, seeing professional golfers playing in a PGA Tour event, wondering exactly when he would get his chance to play that particular tournament.

The year was 1955, and Palmer was a rookie on the PGA Tour with nothing more on his résumé than the 1954 U.S. Amateur title. The course he was sneaking a peek at was Thunderbird Country Club outside Palm Springs, where the Thunderbird Invitational was being played. As a young pro with no real standing on the tour, Palmer had not been given a spot in the invitational tournament. But Palmer and his wife, Winnie, drove to Palm Springs from Brawley near the Mexican border, where Palmer had competed in a smaller tour event. With a small silver trailer hooked up to the car, Palmer had just wanted to see what the Thunderbird tournament and the emerging desert golf scene was about.

Four years later, Palmer would win that Thunderbird Invitational, the first of six official PGA Tour wins in an area that would become a second home for the man most credited with sparking an explosion of interest in golf in the late 1950s and the early 1960s. Palmer was the King of golf, and the Coachella Valley was certainly one of his kingdoms.

The love affair between Palmer and the desert was almost instantaneous.

"I liked the conditions. I thought it was really neat," Palmer said in a 2003 interview. "I liked the golf courses. They were all very well-manicured. The weather was usually nice and warm. The only thing after the first few years, my wife sort of stopped coming. Which was kind of disappointment, but that was the only negative to the whole thing."

By the time Palmer won the 1959 Thunderbird Invitational, he was already establishing himself not just as a top player but as a force of nature. No one in recent memory had come along and captured the imagination of the American sporting public quite like Palmer. Handsome, strong and oozing a kind of blue-collar eastern Pennsylvania charisma, Palmer also had a thunderous game to match his massive public appeal. Palmer swung the golf club with purpose, hammering low draws with every club in his bag.

The classic and powerful follow through of the most popular golfer of his time. A five-time Bob Hope Classic winner, Arnold Palmer loved the desert and has made it a part-time home. *Courtesy of Desert Classic Archives.*

His hands and forearms were so strong that to avoid hooking every shot he had to develop a characteristic blocked follow through, bringing the club twisting up over his head rather than the more classic behind-the-head finish of most pros.

Palmer's smile, his follow through and his advance-at-all-costs, try-to-make-every-shot approach to the game wouldn't have meant much without victories. And Palmer was getting victories. A few months after he looked through the fence at Thunderbird Country Club in 1955, Palmer earned his first tour title at the Canadian Open. He added two more wins in 1956; five more wins in 1957; three wins, including the Masters, in 1958; and three wins in 1959, including the Thunderbird Invitational in the desert. That win featured a final-round 62, a charge from behind that became a kind of trademark for Palmer. The young pro's growing legion of followers dubbed themselves Arnie's Army.

That 1959 win at Thunderbird was historic for more than just Palmer getting his first desert win. The Thunderbird Invitational did wonderful things for the desert and for Thunderbird Country Club. The club itself was now branded as a major hot spot for golf on the West Coast, having hosted the official PGA Tour event as well and the 1955 Ryder Cup. And certainly it didn't hurt that people around the country were learning that Bob Hope, Bing Crosby and Lucille Ball were part of the Thunderbird world.

But the truth was the Thunderbird Invitational also had its problems. First was the purse, just $15,000 by 1959, with $1,500 going to Palmer for the victory. That was low even by 1950s standards for professional golf. The purse for the Los Angeles Open that year, won by Ken Venturi, was $35,000. The Phoenix Open was $20,000. Up the California coast, Art Wall won $4,000 for his victory at the Bing Crosby National Pro-Am in Pebble Beach, a tournament better known as Crosby's Clambake.

There was also some discontent among the members at Thunderbird, who were losing their golf course for a week during the height of what was becoming known in the Coachella Valley as "the season," the time when tourists and part-time residents were in the desert between the end of the fall and the beginning of the summer. The members at other courses in the area, Tamarisk, La Quinta, Eldorado, Bermuda Dunes, Indian Wells and the like, didn't lose their courses during the week of the Thunderbird event.

It all added up to the plain truth that the 1959 Thunderbird Invitational was going to be the last event. And that just didn't sit well with the movers and shakers in the desert golf world as they gathered on the back of the driving range at Thunderbird Country Club during the 1959 Thunderbird

Between them, Arnold Palmer and Jack Nicklaus won three of the first four playings of the tournament first known as the Palm Springs Golf Classic. Palmer won in 1960 and 1962 and Nicklaus won in 1963. *Courtesy of Desert Classic Archives.*

Invitational. It was a kind of Mount Rushmore of important people in the Coachella Valley at the time. Milt Hicks, a member at Thunderbird and an original investor in Indian Wells Country Club, was there. Ernie Dunlevie, the longtime real estate agent and developer of Bermuda Dunes Country Club, was there. The Vines brothers, Ed and Ellsworth, were on hand, as were Johnny Dawson, the developer of Thunderbird Country Club, and Jimmy Hines, now at Eldorado Country Club.

What if, someone tossed out, we could get more than just one golf course involved in the tournament? The desert could keep the dates it has on the tour schedule for 1960. But which courses would be involved? Thunderbird was interested if other courses would join in. Hicks, dubbed Mr. Golf because of his work at Thunderbird, Indian Wells and the desert's two Ryder Cup Matches, assured everyone Indian Wells would be part of the plan. Dunlevie, whose Bermuda Dunes course wouldn't officially open for another few weeks, was naturally interested. Ellsworth Vines said he would get back to the group about Tamarisk being part of what was becoming a far-flung enterprise.

When Tamarisk quickly agreed to be involved as well, the little conversation on the driving range had turned into a four-course extravaganza that would be called the Palm Springs Golf Classic. With four courses in the mix, the Classic would be a five-day, ninety-hole event with a seventy-two-hole cut and a massive pro-am format. It's always interesting to think how the history of the desert and golf might have been different had only three courses agreed to be in the tournament rather than four.

Just how such a tournament could operate was a major consideration. The idea was to have a pro play with a three-player amateur team each of the first four days and then have a cut, with only the pros playing the fifth round on a host course. For help, the tournament turned to one of the smartest players on the tour, 1959 PGA Championship winner Bob Rosburg. Armed with a yellow legal pad and colored pencils, Rosburg locked himself into a cottage at Bermuda Dunes Country Club. Three days later, he came out of the cottage with a format and rotation that would stay with the tournament for more than fifty years.

Palmer won the first Palm Springs Golf Classic in 1960, hosted by Thunderbird, the same course he had won on one year earlier. This time he shot 65 in the final round. Two years later, he won again with a final-round 69 at host course Bermuda Dunes. Palmer was reaching new heights of popularity for golf in the country, having won two majors in 1960 among his eight tour titles. That included his fabled U.S. Open title in 1960 when he rallied from seven shots back in the final round after starting by driving the green on the opening par-four at Cherry Hills Country Club in Denver. He added six wins in 1961, including the British Open. Then in 1962, Palmer won eight more titles, including his third Masters and second British Open titles. With seven wins in 1963, Palmer had twenty-nine wins in four years.

While it helped that Palmer, the best player in the world, was winning the Palm Springs Classic, what few fans knew was how badly the tournament was struggling in its early years. The event had overreached for a $100,000 purse pledge in 1960 based on a promise of a $50,000 television contract that Desi Arnaz believed he had secured for the event. The contract fell through, though, and even cutting the purse to $70,000 ensured that the tournament would lose money. Organizers even went so far as to make up the deficit themselves and take out a loan of $15,000, money they gave away to local charities as alleged profits from the event. By 1964, the tournament was fighting a tax problem based in those struggles in 1960 and faced a $110,000 bill from the Internal Revenue Service. A few high-profile friends and a powerful tax attorney named Dana Latham managed to get the tournament through the storm.

That tax problem had delayed by one year the tournament's plans to bring on a celebrity host. If Arnold Palmer was the best-known professional golfer in the world, then Bob Hope was the best-known amateur golfer in the world. Whether he was on stage, on television or even in his movies, Hope often had a golf club in his hand or was talking about how bad his game was.

"If you think golf is relaxing, you're not doing it right." "Golf is a Four-letter word." "Golf is misery with a caddy."

Hope was a natural to host the desert tournament. He and his wife, Dolores, had bought two homes in Palm Springs in the 1940s, and they were among the first members at Thunderbird Country Club in 1951. Perhaps Hope's friend and co-star in the Road movies, Bing Crosby, would have been a good choice, but Crosby already hosted a tour event on the Monterey Peninsula, a tournament that he had started in the San Diego area before World War II.

But how do you ask one of the busiest entertainers in the world to lend his name to a PGA Tour event and make sure he is in the desert for a week each year as the face of the event? Stories vary a bit on how Hope came to the tournament. Hope's story was that he turned the event down but decided to help organizers by making contact with one of his sponsors, Chrysler. Chrysler executives said they would get involved only if Hope was involved, and Hope relented.

The perpetual trophy for the Hope Classic was called the Eisenhower Trophy and featured a putter from the former president himself. Here Eisenhower (left) and Hope (right) show off the trophy with one of the tournament's founding fathers, Ernie Dunlevie (center). *Courtesy of Desert Classic Archives.*

Another story is that two of the founders of the new tournament, Milt Hicks and Ernie Dunlevie, pursued Hope hard, even tracking him down in the locker room at O'Donnell Golf Course one day to broach the subject. Later, the three men found themselves on the same commuter Western Airlines flight from Palm Springs to Los Angeles. Dunlevie's story was that Hicks worked his way into first class and talked to Hope, who by the end of the flight had agreed to host the event.

But Palmer gives credit to Dunlevie, who had become a friend of the young Palmer in the earliest days of the Palm Springs Classic.

"Ernie Dunlevie was a major contributor to my coming here and a good friend. He became a very close friend," Palmer said. "We had a lot in common. He didn't play a lot of golf then. But we did a lot of eating at the The Nest [a Palm Desert restaurant and bar and a popular Palmer haunt]. He befriended me. He was very nice to me. Whenever I need something here, accommodations or the like, he was there to help me.

Perhaps the most famous vehicle in the Coachella Valley, Bob Hope's famous ski-nosed golf cart. *Courtesy of Desert Classic Archives.*

Of all those major contributors, Ernie stayed. He never backed off. He was the main man."

With the IRS issues out of the way, the Palm Springs Golf Classic became the Bob Hope Desert Classic in 1965. Hope and his connections with golf, entertainment and even politics had an immediate impact. In that first year, Billy Capser won the title by rolling in a two-foot par putt on the final hole at Bermuda Dunes Country Club with Hope and his close friend former president Dwight Eisenhower looking on.

Hope was not one to get involved in the day-to-day details of the tournament. He was far too busy an entertainer for that. But Hope did promote the tournament and its players when he could. He would have Palmer or Gary Player on his NBC specials and go on *The Tonight Show* with Johnny Carson to promote the event the week of the tournament. And he would play in the event, which in itself brought fans out from the desert and made the tournament one of the most popular golf events on television.

Bob Hope used to call Jackie Gleason (left) one of his favorite pigeons. Gleason would remind Hope what pigeons do to people. *Courtesy of Desert Classic Archives.*

"Hope was a friend of a lot of the older guys, even before I came on the scene," Palmer recalled in the 2003 interview. "He played in the Crosby some. But Bob Hope was always, as long as I knew him, an avid golfer. We became pretty good friends. I did a movie with him, I played golf with him a lot."

One of Palmer's favorite stories was playing a pro-am with Hope in the Phoenix Open. Somehow the afternoon turned into a day of sleet and

Popular culture was always part of the Bob Hope Classic. Here Hope interviews astronaut Alan Shepard, who hit a golf ball on the moon. *Courtesy of Desert Classic Archives.*

rain. But Palmer said Hope shot a thirty-five on his own ball on the back nine, and the Palmer-Hope team won the pro-am. Hope was a fine player but always seemed just a step behind his friend Crosby, who won club titles at Thunderbird and Eldorado in the desert and Lakeside Country Club in Los Angeles.

Hope was able to do for the desert tournament what Crosby had done for the Pebble Beach event. The desert's tournament always featured the celebrities who lived in the Coachella Valley, but Hope was able to pick up a phone and get his famous friends from outside the desert to play. Suddenly, the pro-am featured Kirk Douglas, Dean Martin and Sammy Davis Jr. The pros respected Hope, so they came to the desert more and more. And Hope's sense of giving the public what it wanted meant he always had something up his sleeve for the pro-am. He loved to have astronauts, widely considered American heroes, in his tournament. He would bring along gag celebrities, like Phyllis Diller and Irene Ryan, Granny from *The Beverly Hillbillies*, as his personal caddy. College football coaches and professional athletes were suddenly in the pro-am. Pretty much every celebrity in Hollywood would make an appearance or two in Hope's tournament, except for one. Bing Crosby never played in the event.

Crosby, who lived above Thunderbird Country Club ("up the hill") in an area officially known as Thunderbird Heights, was always a slightly better golfer than his friend Hope. But while Hope saw the need to play to the gallery with his pro-am, Crosby wanted serious golf in his tournament. Yes, some fun celebrities always played in the Crosby, but Crosby didn't have as much tolerance for the kind of gags that happened in the Hope Classic. So while Hope played in the Crosby, Crosby never played in the Hope.

That serious nature of Crosby certainly came through in one of the rituals just before the Hope tournament, a match between Arnold Palmer and Milt Hicks on one side and pro Bo Wininger and Crosby on the other. Palmer is not the first person to recall that when the match was over and Crosby's side was down and owed a few dollars to the other team. Well, the match wasn't really over. Crosby would insist that the match go to a nineteenth hole, or a twentieth or twenty-first. The sides would play until Crosby got back to even or until there was too little light to continue the match. Crosby never liked to pay.

Another area where Hope had helped the desert tournament was that the event was now broadcast nationally on NBC, which would be Hope's home on radio and television for six decades. Hope's presence brought more money from NBC for the broadcast rights. Ernie Dunlevie said the tournament's fee

Glen Campbell hosted the PGA Tour event at Riviera Country Club in Los Angeles for a few years, but he was also a mainstay in the Bob Hope Classic. *Courtesy of Desert Classic Archives.*

from NBC jumped from $50,000 in 1964 to $100,000 with Hope in 1965. That helped jump-start the tournament's purse. When Tommy Jacobs won the 1964 Palm Springs Classic at Eldorado Country Club, the purse was $50,000. When Billy Capser won in 1965 with the Hope name on the event, the purse was $80,000.

As the Bob Hope Classic grew, so did Palmer's role in the tournament and in the desert. Now a part-time desert resident along with his homes in Latrobe, Pennsylvania, and Florida, Palmer remained a threat every time he teed up in the desert. He lost a chance at a third Hope title in 1966 when he fell in a playoff to Doug Sanders at Indian Wells Country Club. But in 1968, Palmer was on the other side of a playoff, beating a good player with bigger things in his future off the golf course, future PGA Tour Commissioner Deane Beman.

By 1971, Palmer was winning less frequently, but he still managed a win in the Hope Classic, beating Ray Floyd in a playoff at Bermuda Dunes. It would be two full years before Palmer, who was forty-three at the 1973 Hope Classic, won again. While the 1973 Classic would be the last of Palmer's sixty-two wins on the tour, it had to be one of the sweetest. Palmer entered the final round at Bermuda Dunes Country Club locked in a tight duel with

The eighteenth hole at Bermuda Dunes Country Club was the site of Arnold Palmer's last PGA Tour victory in 1973 at the Bob Hope Classic. *Courtesy of Graeme Baxter Golf Art.*

rising star Johnny Miller and veteran John Schlee and one shot behind the best player on the tour, Jack Nicklaus. Nicklaus had himself won the Classic in 1963 in an 18-hole playoff over Gary Player, shooting 65 in the playoff at Indian Wells Country Club that made the event a 108-hole event.

Nicklaus and Palmer, friends and rivals since Nicklaus beat Palmer in a playoff in the 1962 U.S. Open at Oakmont Country Club just miles from Palmer's Latrobe home, were in the final threesome with Schlee, who joked that he had come along to referee the match. On a rare rainy day in the desert, Palmer birdied the opening par-five while Nicklaus bogeyed the hole. Palmer had the lead, and he never gave it up. Palmer made the critical putts he needed in the round, and Nicklaus missed some short putts on the back nine, including a three-footer on the sixteenth hole. On the eighteenth green, with Palmer leading by two shots, Nicklaus missed a long eagle putt that could have forced a momentary tie. But Palmer rolled in his own birdie on the hole to secure his fifth Hope Classic win and his sixth PGA Tour win in the desert in fifteen years dating back to the 1959 Thunderbird event.

Andy Williams (left) not only played on the Bob Hope tournament more than any other celebrity but was also a La Quinta Country Club homeowner and hosted his own PGA Tour event in San Diego for two decades. Williams shares a laugh here with professional Lee Trevino. *Courtesy of Desert Classic Archives.*

Asked in 2003 if any of his wins in the Classic stood out, Palmer said he remembers shooting thirty-two on the back nine to catch and pass Gene Littler in 1962.

"And I remember beating Jack," Palmer said, flashing his famous grin. "I liked that."

The Hope and Crosby tournaments were among the most popular on the tour in the 1960s, not only with players but also with television viewers. Many fans would have rather watched the Hope tournament than any of the men's major champions, and the ratings proved it. And that had a long-term impact on the desert, said a man who would become a major course and housing developer in the desert in the 1970s and beyond.

"I have always thought the Rose Bowl and the Bob Hope Classic were the two greatest advertisements for the great weather we have in Southern California," said developer Bill Bone. "Because here on New Year's Day and later January when the tournament was played, they see people walking around in short sleeve golf shirts and sunshine as far as you can see and flowers in bloom and bougainvillea and they are back in the Midwest and nothing is in bloom and they look around [at] all the dead trees and everything and snow up to their knees, and the desert looks pretty good."

The Bob Hope Classic and Arnold Palmer were now forever linked as desert golf icons. And their popularity and having the entire country see them on television in perfect weather in the winter no doubt had much to do with the golf boom that was about to come to the desert in the next two decades.

CHAPTER 6
Playground of the Presidents

Dwight Eisenhower had a cold, and it wasn't going away.

The president of the United States had picked up the cold, according to his press secretary, just as he was returning from a trip to Europe in August 1959. Now it was late September, and the cold was still bothering the chief executive, who was weeks away from his sixty-ninth birthday. So Eisenhower decided to make good on a promise he had made five years earlier. He was going to return to the Coachella Valley to play a little golf and try to kick the cold in the warm desert sunshine.

"That's the kind of weather the president's doctors have advised to shake off the cold," press secretary James Hagerty announced.

Whether it was just trying to get rid of a cold or a chance to pursue his favorite activity, golf, Eisenhower came to the desert for an eight-day vacation starting with his arrival on September 30. While presidents visiting the Coachella Valley dated back to Herbert Hoover, it was Eisenhower who would help the area gain the reputation of a playground for presidents, both those in office and those who made the area a retirement home.

Starting with that eight-day visit in late 1959, just over a year from when his second term in office would end, Dwight Eisenhower had a huge impact on golf in the desert. That shouldn't be a surprise, since Eisenhower, the nation's First Golfer, had done as much as anyone to help the game grow in the United States in the 1950s.

Golf skyrocketed in popularity in the country for a variety of reasons in the decade. There was Bob Hope, likely the most famous entertainer in the world

President Dwight Eisenhower shoots a look toward his vice president, Richard Nixon, as the two play Thunderbird Country Club in 1954. Eisenhower would later become a desert resident, living at Eldorado Country Club in Indian Wells. *Courtesy of Thunderbird Country Club.*

who continued to embrace the game and use it as an important part of his act on stage, on film and on television. There was new professional Arnold Palmer, who was thrilling galleries by trying to overpower courses and winning important tournaments. There was television, which was starting to capture Palmer and the other pros of the day and beaming the images across the country.

But without question, one of the important reasons for the game's popularity was Eisenhower. Once he took office in 1953, Eisenhower made no attempt to conceal his love of the game. He had a putting green installed on the lawn of the White House. He played many rounds of golf in the Washington, D.C. area while in office, especially at Burning Tree Country Club in Bethesda, Maryland, just moments from the White House. As a member of Augusta National Golf Club in Georgia, home of the Masters, Eisenhower had made such a fuss over trying to get a tree taken out of the seventeenth fairway that the club decided to keep the tree but named it after Eisenhower.

As the supreme commander of Allied troops during World War II, Eisenhower had helped guide the United States and Europe to victory. As president, Eisenhower oversaw economic growth in the country but had to handle the issues of the growing cold war. As a golfer, he was devoted and a decent player.

Eisenhower's first venture into the desert came in 1954 at Thunderbird Country Club at the invitation of Paul Helm, a Los Angeles businessman who was also a member of the desert country club. Joining Eisenhower for the round was Eisenhower's young vice president, a former congressman from California named Richard Nixon. Both men would play golf in the desert for years into the future.

Eisenhower also played a round in that first visit at Tamarisk Country Club. The local paper displayed a photograph of Eisenhower with a smiling Ben Hogan and Helm.

But that short 1954 trip might have been the end of Eisenhower's connections to the desert if it hadn't been for that pesky cold and the friendship of Washington, D.C. lawyer George Allen. Allen, who had actually worked for Democratic presidents before forming a friendship with Eisenhower, owned a home in La Quinta and hosted the president. He also took the president to play Eldorado Country Club, where he played for the first time on October 1, 1959. Eisenhower was so enchanted by the desert in general and Eldorado in particular that he decided to spend part of his retirement years at the club. It was arranged for Eisenhower and his wife, Mamie, to be honorary members at Eldorado and live in one of the cottages at the course during their annual stays in the area, which lasted about three months each year. Eisenhower already had several friends in the area, including Allen, former radio star Freeman Gosden of the *Amos 'n' Andy* show and, of course, Bob Hope.

Hope recalled in one of his autobiographies that he first met Eisenhower when Hope was touring northern Africa with his USO show during World War II. Hope was summoned to meet with Eisenhower, who began the

President Dwight Eisenhower lived at Eldorado Country Club in the final years of his presidency and for the remainder of his life. Here Eisenhower chats with reporters during one of his desert visits. *Courtesy of Desert Classic Archives.*

conversation by asking, "How's your golf game?" The two were fast friends from that moment.

Eisenhower's trips to the desert continued through the 1960s. He even scored his only hole in one in the area. That came on February 6, 1968, at Seven Lakes Country Club, an executive course that had been developed by Johnny Dawson.

But Eisenhower had another major impact on the desert and its golf scene that had nothing to do with his own game. For all the great golf and the laughs that came from the Bob Hope Classic in the 1960s, the tournament had a serious side, too. As the desert grew, so did the need for healthcare, particularly in the area around where many of the private country clubs had been built in the mid-valley that would become Rancho Mirage, Indian Wells and Palm Desert. If someone suffered, say, a heart attack at one of those clubs, it was a long ride to a hospital in Palm Springs on the west end of the valley or Indio on the east end of the valley.

Above: Dolores Hope was always a part of the golf action in the desert and was the first president of Eisenhower Medical Center's board of directors. Here, Dolores helps her husband present the Eisenhower Trophy to 1977 winner Hubert Green as fans climb the rocks to get a better view. *Courtesy of Desert Classic Archives.*

Right: Bob and Dolores Hope were not just the most famous couple in the desert but among the most active in charity work as well. *Courtesy of International Management Group.*

The organizers of the Hope Classic, called the Palm Springs Golf Classic in its first five years, decided that proceeds from the tournament should go toward building some kind of medical facility in the central part of the desert. When approached about the idea of putting his name on the facility, Eisenhower agreed. That, in turned, upped the expectations of what the mid-valley medical facility should be. So was born the Eisenhower Medical Center in Rancho Mirage. Plans for the hospital began in the early 1960s with Dolores Hope saying she was volunteered by her husband to be chair of the board of directors. The eighty acres for the hospital was donated by Bob and Dolores Hope on a road that was later renamed Bob Hope Drive.

As plans and construction progressed on the medical center, Eisenhower made numerous appearances at Hope's tournament throughout the 1960s, often handing out the tournament's perpetual trophy, called the Eisenhower Trophy and featuring a mounted putter from the president. Eisenhower had friends on the tour, but none closer than the man who won the desert event five times, Arnold Palmer.

President Dwight Eisenhower congratulates 1967 Bob Hope Classic winner Tom Nieporte, who edged Doug Sanders for the title. Tournament host Bob Hope looks on. *Courtesy of Desert Classic Archives.*

"Actually, I had met him at Ligonier in Pennsylvania at a centennial celebration or something like that for Ligonier," Palmer recalled in a 2003 interview. "And then I won the Masters in '58, and that's when I got to know him pretty well. That's when I started to play golf with him, in '58."

Palmer was a frequent guest at the Eisenhower's home on the eleventh fairway at Eldorado, sitting and talking with the former president who preferred to be called "General" rather than "Mr. President."

Eisenhower would never see the completed hospital. Plagued by heart issues dating back to his first term in office as president, Eisenhower eventually suffered four heart attacks and spent much of the last year of his life in Walter Reed Medical Center in Washington, D.C. Eisenhower died on March 28, 1969, of congestive heart failure at Walter Reed. Two days later, on March 30, golfers at all Coachella Valley golf courses were

Early construction on what would become the Eisenhower Medical Center in Rancho Mirage. Much of the money to build the medical complex came from proceeds from the Bob Hope Classic. *Courtesy of Desert Classic Archives.*

requested to stop play at 11:00 a.m. and observe three minutes of silence for the former supreme commander of Allied forces, former president and the desert's most famous golfer.

While in the desert, Eisenhower would play from time to time at the private nine-hole course just up the road from where the Eisenhower Medical Center would be built in what is now Rancho Mirage. Called Sunnylands, the course and surrounding estate were owned by publishing magnate and Eisenhower friend Walter Annenberg and his wife, Leonore. Always active in politics, Annenberg was later the U.S. ambassador to England under President Richard Nixon.

The Sunnylands course was built in 1963 but only after a long struggle over water rights for the course. The course features an innovative design by architect Dick Wilson, who would go on to design Cog Hill No. 4 in Chicago and the original Blue Monster Course at Doral Country Club in Miami. Rather than just replaying the nine holes from a different set of tees to complete an eighteen-hole round, Wilson designed a course that at times seemed like a cross-country affair. The green for the par-three fourth hole, for instance, is used for two other holes, the par-four tenth and the par-three thirteenth. The fairway for the third hole is also used for the eleventh and twelfth holes. It's a little bit like a snake swallowing its own tail.

As it was a completely private course, Annenberg could invite whomever he wished to play with him. Eisenhower played and once noted that the course had no palm trees. Annenberg planted two palms on the second hole in Eisenhower's honor.

But other presidents played the course, too. Richard Nixon played Sunnylands a few times during his presidency and even after he had resigned from office in 1974. Bill Clinton played the course before he was elected president in 1992. Gerald Ford, who had succeeded Nixon, played the course often. But it was Ronald Reagan whose trips to Sunnylands were among the most high profile. Reagan came to the Rancho Mirage estate while governor of California and then would make many trips to Sunnylands over the New Year's holidays while he was president. It was a perfect place for a president to get away, with a nine-hole course inside the high oleander hedges that would eventually be replaced by a high pink wall.

One of Annenberg's presidential guests would become the second former president to call the Coachella Valley a permanent home. Gerald Ford was a naturally gifted athlete, playing center for the University of Michigan football team long before he was elected to the U.S. House of Representatives as a Republican from Grand Rapids in 1948. Golf was never really part of

After his presidency ended in 1977, Gerald Ford settled into Thunderbird Country Club as a snowbird resident. Here, Ford, along with club president Robert Booth, cuts the ribbon after the course was remodeled. *Courtesy of Thunderbird Country Club.*

Ford's athletic life, though, unless you count his days of caddying for his stepfather as a youth.

As a politician, Ford would rise to minority leader of the House. When Spiro Agnew resigned as Richard Nixon's vice president in October 1972, Nixon selected Ford to become the vice president. Ford was a popular choice and very well liked among all members of the Congress. When Nixon resigned because of the Watergate scandal on August 8, 1974, Ford ascended to the presidency.

Perhaps from fatigue over the Watergate issues, perhaps because Ford had pardoned Nixon, perhaps because Ford had reached the presidency without running for either vice president or president, Ford lost the 1976 presidential election to Democrat Jimmy Carter. That left Ford and his wife, Betty, a decision to make: where to retire? The Fords felt Florida and the Monterey Peninsula in California were too humid for Betty's arthritis. The Coachella Valley was warm and dry and was full of friends of the Fords, like longtime

President Gerald Ford, fresh from leaving the White House in 1977, accepts his membership at Thunderbird Country Club. The Fords purchased two homes at the club, one as a home and one as a suite of offices for the former president. *Courtesy of Thunderbird Country Club.*

friends Bob and Dolores Hope. Leonard Firestone, who led the family-founded Firestone Tire and Rubber and who had been U.S. ambassador to Belgium under both Nixon and Ford, had built four homes at Thunderbird Country Club. Two had been left unoccupied, as Firestone wanted to select the people who lived in the house. Those people turned out to be Gerry and Betty Ford, with one house used as a residence and the other used as a suite of offices for the former president.

Ford dove head first into golf after his presidency. When he left Washington, he flew to Pebble Beach to play in Bing Crosby's event the next

Former president Gerald Ford shakes hands with Thunderbird president Ralph Phinney as Ford becomes a member of the club in 1977. *Courtesy of Thunderbird Country Club.*

day. Three weeks later, he played in his first Bob Hope Classic. Ford would become a fixture in the event, as much as Hope or Arnold Palmer. Ford would generally play with Hope and another amateur, sometimes a celebrity, often Ford's friend Representative Thomas P. "Tip" O'Neill. O'Neill was one of numerous politicians who would play in the Hope, a list that included two sitting vice presidents, Spiro Agnew and Dan Quayle, as well as senators and representatives from both side of the political aisle.

While Hope routinely filleted Ford and his golf game, Ford would find ways to fire back.

"The truth is you have made a shambles out of any reputation I might have had as a senior statesmen," Ford said in his welcoming letter for the 1994

Former president Gerald Ford tees off on the first hole of one of his earliest rounds as a member at Thunderbird Country Club. *Courtesy of Thunderbird Country Club.*

Classic. People in Europe, Japan, Hong Kong, Mexico as well as the United States laugh at me because of the things you've said about my golf game."

Hope and Ford couldn't help but throw jabs at each other. Hope would point out that Ford could lose a ball in a ball washer. Ford would ask Hope what it was like to entertain the troops at Gettysburg.

Bob Hope loved to have politicians in his Classic tournament. In 1970, Vice President Spiro Agnew (far left) hit his playing partner, Doug Sanders, in the back of the head with a shot at La Quinta Country Club. Sanders and Agnew became close friends. *Courtesy of Desert Classic Archives.*

Former president Gerald Ford was popular among fans and PGA Tour golfers. Here Ford talked to Champions Tour pro Dave Stockton. *Courtesy of Thunderbird Country Club.*

The Bob Hope Classic brought together big names from various segments of life. Here, from left, former president George H.W. Bush, former president Gerald Ford, sitting president Bill Clinton and singer Glen Campbell share a laugh at Indian Wells Country Club in 1995. *Courtesy of Desert Classic Archives.*

Ford continued to play in the tournament well into the 1990s, despite having both knees replaced. And he would be part of the surprising zenith of the presidential influence on golf in the desert. That came on February 15, 1995, a day when not one, not two, but three presidents came together to play in the first round of the Bob Hope Chrysler Classic.

The group naturally included Ford, a fixture in the Hope tournament even as he struggled with bad knees. The surprise was that Hope's pull on the political world convinced both former president George H.W. Bush and sitting president Bill Clinton to join Ford for the round of golf to be played at Indian Wells Country Club. The three presidents would be joined by Hope himself and the defending champion of the tournament, Scott Hoch, to form the tournament's first-ever First Fivesome.

It was a fitting tribute to Hope that three men who had held the highest office in the land were joining together to play in his tournament while benefitting a hospital named after another former president, Dwight Eisenhower. After all, Hope had been a great pal of Eisenhower, and no one could question the comedian's dedication to the country and to its

It was a tribute to Bob Hope (second from right) that he was able to get three presidents to play in his tournament in 1995. Here Hope stands with George H.W. Bush, Bill Clinton and Gerald Ford. The day might have been one of the last times Hope played eighteen full holes, at the age of ninety-one. *Courtesy of Desert Classic Archives.*

servicemen and women through his tireless touring efforts in touring foreign lands for the USO.

Still, there was a bit of shock in the grouping. It had been just twenty-eight months since Clinton, a Democrat, had beaten the Republican Bush in the 1992 general election, turning Bush into a one-term president. And it was known that there was not a tremendous warmth between Bush and Clinton. That would change drastically through the years, with Clinton and Bush becoming great friends. But in 1995, how could anyone, even Bob Hope, have convinced the two political rivals to play in the same fivesome?

Quickly and quietly, the story spread through the desert that perhaps the tournament organizers had not been completely honest with Bush. They might just have said that Bush would play in the same round with Clinton and Ford, but not told him the plan was to have Bush and Clinton play together in the same fivesome. Ernie Dunlevie, a longtime board member of the tournament, would later confirm that he had received a call from his own close friend, Arnold Palmer, who was talking to Bush. It fell to Dunlevie

While there may have been some lingering ill feelings between George H.W. Bush and Bill Clinton from the 1992 election during their 1995 round at the Hope Classic, the two would eventually become close friends through their work for disaster relief across the world. *Courtesy of Desert Classic Archives.*

to tell Palmer and Bush that yes, Bush was slated to play with the man who had beaten him just over two years earlier.

It would not have been a surprise if Bush had pulled out of the group given the new knowledge that he would play with Clinton. But Bush decided to uphold his commitment to the tournament and play in what had to be one of the most widely covered days of golf in the desert. Not only did the golf media from across the country come to the event for the fabulous day of three presidents, but national media and the White House press corps also decided on Indian Wells for the round. Estimates are that more than twenty thousand people showed up to the small, tight Indian Wells Country Club course to watch the fivesome, with plenty of Secret Service and other security quite visible.

The day turned into a triumph for the tournament, with the three presidents laughing and joking throughout the day and Hope insisting that he stay out for the entire round rather than come in for a few holes as had become his habit in the tournament in recent years. Hoch survived with a 2-under 70, a rather average round on the short Indian Wells course. But what other pro had ever played with three presidents? The only complaint came from Bush, a notoriously fast player, who complained that the pace of play was too slow.

George H.W. Bush had been beaten for reelection to the presidency by Bill Clinton in 1992, but in 1995, Bush and Clinton played together at Indian Wells Country Club in the Bob Hope Classic. *Courtesy of Desert Classic Archives.*

"I do remember even though I was just as wild as Bush and Ford were, I was the only person who didn't hit anybody with an errant golf ball," Clinton laughed on the twentieth anniversary of the famous round. "I was ragging them. I said, you know, that's us Democrats. We are a little softhearted. We go easy on the crowd."

It should be noted that Clinton and Bush, two of the major figures in that famous day in the Hope Classic, would grow to become longtime friends after each was out of the Oval Office.

No one at the time could possibly have known that seventeen years later, with Hope's tournament in serious danger of disappearing, Clinton would be one of the key figures in rescuing the event. The Hope Classic had lost tournament

When Bill Clinton played in the first round of the 1995 Bob Hope Classic, he was the first sitting president to play in a PGA Tour pro-am event. *Courtesy of Desert Classic Archives.*

sponsor Chrysler after the 2008 event as car manufacturers were hit hard by the recession of the time. Without a title sponsor, the same format that was quirky in the 1960s but no longer popular among the pros and a field devoid of the top players in the game, a new partnership arose for the event after the 2011 tournament. Part of that partnership was the Clinton Foundation, which would help turn the event into a forum for health and wellness, along with new sponsor Humana, a Louisville, Kentucky healthcare provider. Clinton was brought into the partnership by his old friend PGA Tour commissioner Tim Finchem.

Clinton would serve as a kind of host for the event, host a health conference during the week and annually make sure that fans didn't forget the legacy of Bob Hope.

During one visit to the desert's PGA Tour event, Clinton joked that he wanted to get on one of the desert's high-profile golf courses.

"I'll have to call W. I understand he has an honorary membership there," Clinton said, referring to George W. Bush. Another golfing president, Barack Obama, has made four trips to the desert in just three years from 2013 to 2015. Twice Obama stayed at Annenberg's Sunnylands, getting in rounds of golf between meetings with the president of China and the king of Jordan. On Valentine's Day 2014 and 2015, Obama came to the desert on no greater pretense than to play golf on a quick vacation with friends from Hawaii, either at Sunnylands or another ultra-private eighteen-hole course called Porcupine Creek in Rancho Mirage, owned by Oracle founder Larry Ellison.

As one lasting legacy to presidents in the desert, the desert's PGA Tour event has raised $54 million for desert charities, including $34 million for the Eisenhower Medical Center. The legacy of golf, the desert and presidents seems more than secure.

CHAPTER 7
The Ladies Play Through

David Foster wanted to sell soap. At least, he wanted to sell more soap and related products than his Colgate-Palmolive company was selling as the 1970s rolled around.

What Colgate-Palmolive's products needed, Foster felt, was a platform that could speak directly to the demographic that bought his toothpaste and dishwashing soap and other products. Sports might be a good idea, women's sports in particular, he thought.

Foster had been a highly decorated Royal Navy officer in World War II, and he even wrote a book about his wartime experiences. He later married the English actress Glynis Johns in 1952, but they divorced after just a few years. In 1946, he joined Colgate-Palmolive as a management trainee at the company in 1946. He rose steadily through the management ranks and was eventually elected president of Colgate-Palmolive in 1970, about the time he was looking around for the right sport to help market his products.

Women's tennis at the time was dominated by cigarette brand Virginia Slims. Foster, an admitted golf nut, thought that women's golf was underutilized as a marketing platform for sponsors. But Foster couldn't have just another tournament with just another $25,000 purse on the LPGA Tour. He would have to have a big, important tournament that fans would notice.

So began one of the biggest events in golf in the Coachella Valley. Foster, along with his handpicked hostess, singer and television personality Dinah Shore, gave the LPGA its premier event in 1972 with the Colgate Dinah Shore

When David Foster asked Dinah Shore to be the hostess of a new tournament in the desert of Southern California, she thought he meant a tennis tournament. Shore didn't play golf at the time but ended up becoming the only non-player in the LPGA Hall of Fame. *Courtesy of International Management Group.*

Winner's Circle tournament at a fledgling course in Rancho Mirage called Mission Hills Country Club. It was a tournament that would redefine the LPGA and make the Coachella Valley the center of the women's golf world.

"If it wasn't for David Foster we wouldn't be where we are today, really," said LPGA Hall of Famer and Coachella Valley resident Marlene Hagge. "Because that was the kind of the jump that made a difference. The course was being built at the time. David came right in, and he did so much for women's golf."

The Colgate Dinah Shore Winner's Circle had much to offer women's golf, from its record $110,000 purse to national television coverage and a host that most of the country knew and liked. But that 1972 debut on the Desmond Muirhead–designed course at Mission Hills Country Club was far from the first time the top female golfers in the country had played the desert courses. The truth was that years before "the Dinah" started being played, women's golf had a starring role in the Coachella Valley.

Even before Helen Dettweiler designed a nine-hole course for her friend aviatrix Jackie Cochran in 1946, female golfers were getting the advantages of the desert's growing golf scene. Mostly that came from O'Donnell Golf Course in Palm Springs. That nine-hole course began the Palm Springs Golf Invitational for the top amateur men golfers on the West Coast in 1936. In the same year, O'Donnell also conducted a Palm Springs Women's Golf Invitational. These were strictly amateur affairs, since professional golf for men was barely recognized as legitimate in the 1920s and 1930s. Women certainly didn't play golf for money in those times, at least not in polite society.

That was changing in the 1940s when Dettweiler was trying to help form a Women's PGA professional circuit. That circuit never took off, but players like Patty Berg were trying to find a way to make a living at professional golf in post–World War II America.

It all was inspiring younger golfers like Marlene Bauer (later Hagge) and her elder sister Alice to dream of making a living in professional golf. Hagge won two big amateur events in the desert in 1948, the tournament at Cochran-Odlum Ranch in Indio and the Palm Springs Women's Golf Invitational at O'Donnell. Hagge was just fourteen at the time and still two years away from being one of the founders of the Ladies Professional Golf Association, or LPGA.

Hagge and her elder sister Alice found a patron of sorts in their early years in the Los Angeles and desert areas, Dolores Hope.

"It was funny. In those days it was tough to be a golfer if you were a girl. They didn't allow women on some of the snitzy courses in L.A.," Hagge said. "They wouldn't allow children under 16 to play in the California State Amateur, L.A. City and so forth. So she would take us to play, and she would take Alice and me to play these courses, and of course no one could say no to her. The L.A. Country Club and Bel Air, she was very instrumental. She was really the only reason I was able to play in these tournaments in the desert."

Four years before Hagge's win at O'Donnell, the tournament had perhaps its most famous winner. Babe Didrikson Zaharias was already known as the world's greatest female athlete thanks to her fame in basketball, baseball and softball and two gold medals and one silver medal in the 1932 Olympic Games in Los Angeles. Zaharias was now focused on golf and already had won the 1940 Western Open, considered a women's major title at the time.

The United States Golf Association had ruled Zaharias a professional because she had earned money in other sports. But in January 1944, Zaharias had her amateur status reinstated. The same was true of Coachella Valley legend Johnny Dawson, whom the USGA refused to let play in its national events because he held at job as a salesman for a sporting goods company.

The amateur status allowed Zaharias to play in the 1944 O'Donnell event, and she showed her brilliance with a two-round total of 143, 1 shot better than the tournament record and eleven shots ahead of her nearest competition. Zaharias won the second of her three Western Open titles later that year. By 1948, playing as a pro, she won the U.S. Women's Open for the first time.

After Hagge's win in 1948, another player with desert connections won the O'Donnell. Beverly Hanson and her family had moved from Fargo, North Dakota, to Indio, where the young Hanson took lessons from Helen Dettweiler. Hanson blossomed into one of the top amateurs in the country and was winning events across the United States. In the Palm Springs tournament in 1950, she hammered the field by fourteen shots. A year later, Hanson turned pro and won her first LPGA start, setting a fifty-four-hole scoring record of 213 in the Women's Eastern Open in Redding, Pennsylvania. It was the first of sixteen LPGA wins for Hanson, including three majors, before she retired, was married, had twins and settled into a long run as the teaching professional at Eldorado Country Club in Indian Wells.

Zaharias, Dettweiler, Hagge and her sister Alice were among the thirteen golfers who founded the LPGA in 1950. Over the next two decades, the LPGA would find a home in the desert, even if not all of the LPGA's appearances were official events.

The first official LPGA event in the desert came in 1953 at Tamarisk Country Club. The Palm Springs Open was ballyhooed as having all the top women players for the two-day event, including the great Zaharias. But by the time the event rolled around on April 15 and 16, the talk was of Zaharias not playing because of a diagnosis of cancer. Zaharias would recover briefly, even winning a U.S. Women's Open in 1954 after her surgery. But Zaharias died in September 1956 with ten career major titles, four won as an amateur. She was among the first six players inducted into the LPGA Hall of Fame in 1967.

Without Zaharias, the Palm Springs Open was still played, with Hawaiian star Jackie Pung taking the victory by two shots over Betsey Rawls. Pung earned $750 from the $3,000 purse, but Rawls would reverse the leaderboard later that year, edging Pung at the U.S. Women's Open.

The exhibitions in the desert might not have been official, but the money was real for the LPGA players who were trying hard to keep their association growing and thriving.

"We would go to a course and we would do everything ourselves," Hagge recalled. "We would pound the out-of-bound stakes and we had our own scoring committee. It was just us doing it to keep the tour going."

The next big but unofficial LPGA event in the desert didn't come until 1967, and it was a one-day tournament on an executive golf course called Seven Lakes Country Club in Palm Springs. Par on the course was 58, and the $4,000 purse for the Seven Lakes Invitational wasn't bad for an eighteen-hole event. The winner was certainly not surprising. Mickey Wright was already establishing herself as perhaps the greatest female golfer of all time. A young prodigy from San Diego, Wright had made a name for herself in the Coachella Valley by winning a big amateur title, the Thunderbird Women's Invitational, in 1952 when she was just seventeen but already a freshman at Stanford University. The next year, for good measure, Wright won the Thunderbird title again. By 1955, she had turned professional, and in 1957, she started a streak of fourteen years with at least one LPGA victory, the second-longest streak in LPGA history. In the middle of that streak, it was common for Wright to win seven or eight tournaments a year, with one or two being major championships. She earned four year-end money titles and five Vare scoring trophies. No less an authority than Ben Hogan said Wright had the finest swing in golf. Not the finest women's swing. The finest swing, period.

At Seven Lakes in 1967, Wright fired a 7-under 51 to take the title by 2 shots over three other players. A year later, it was Sharon Miller who won the title with a 5-under 53, again with a $4,000 purse and $600 first prize. But just four weeks later, on November 1–3, the biggest (and this time official) LPGA event in desert history was played at Canyon Country Club in Palm Springs, and it was won by another all-time great.

Kathy Whitworth might not have been considered as great a player as Mickey Wright, but Whitworth's numbers stand up to any player. She won eighty-eight career titles, six more than Wright. Whitworth won seven of the first eight LPGA Player of the Year awards, an honor started in 1966. She also won seven Vare trophies for the low-scoring average of the year. And while Wright had a fourteen-year winning streak, Whitworth won at least one title in seventeen straight years. Wright might have been hampered by her feet and issues with flying, but Whitworth was an all-time star.

One of those eighty-eight wins came in 1968 at the Canyon Ladies Classic, which boasted a huge purse of $22,750. Whitworth completed three days of the par-72 course in 2-over 218, 2 shots better than three

Kathy Whitworth won the second official LPGA event in the desert at Canyon Country Club in Palm Springs, four years before the Colgate Dinah Shore debuted. *Courtesy of International Management Group.*

other players. Whitworth earned $3,300 for the win, but it would be the last official money the LPGA would hand out in the desert until 1972. But it was that 1972 event that helped change the face of the LPGA. And it also gave the LPGA a new face, that of Dinah Shore.

The story sounds too crazy, too scripted to believe, the kind of legend that Hollywood public relations departments use to build up their stars. But in this case, the legend is true. When singer, actress and television personality Dinah Shore agreed to host a tournament at Mission Hills Country Club in Rancho Mirage, she really did think it was a tennis tournament at first. Because who would ask a non-golfer like Shore to host a golf tournament? Well, David Foster would ask. Foster's Colgate-

Tournament hostess Dinah Shore (left) became great friends with many LPGA stars, including 1977 winner Kathy Whitworth. *Courtesy of International Management Group.*

Palmolive company was a major sponsor of Shore's daytime talk show, *Dinah's Place.*

"She had played a little bit as a kid," said Terry Wilcox, who a decade later would be Shore's friend and swing coach and, later still, the tournament director of Shore's LPGA event. "Her mother was a golfer, so she played as a kid. But when she went to college she didn't [play] any after that until she started playing [for the tournament]. The story is David Foster wanted her to be the hostess of this tournament and she thought it was a tennis tournament. But she took the assignment, and when she found out it was golf she didn't feel like she could back out. So she had to run out and start taking lessons, which she did over in L.A."

Born Frances Rose Shore, Dinah came by her southern drawl honestly, being born in Tennessee. Shore had been a major solo singing artist in the 1940s and 1950s, and she hosted *The Dinah Shore Show*, a variety show in the late 1950s and into the 1960s. That show allowed her to sing a jingle that would become synonymous with her, "See the U-S-A in your Chevrolet." But it was her talk shows that put Shore on television each day and made her one of the most popular and recognizable faces in entertainment.

Shore found friends in the LPGA and not just because she was willing to sponsor one of their biggest events. It was nearly impossible to dislike Shore and her warm, genuinely friendly personality. As the LPGA began its third decade, the women's game still needed all the cheerleaders it could get. Shore was the biggest and the loudest of those cheerleaders. And she was a devoted golfer, Wilcox recalled.

"She was a very, very avid golfer," Wilcox said. "When we got here in 1981, I started working with her. She would stay down here the better part of five months, and she wanted to play or hit balls every day. And she would pretty much play with anybody. She would go over to the starter and ask if there was a game and he would put her with somebody and she would go out and play with them. And all of a sudden they thought that Dinah was the best friend they ever had."

Shore was just part of Foster's plan for garnering attention for his new tournament. First, there had to be national television. Foster and tournament organizers worked out a deal with the Hughes Broadcasting Network to televise the event and syndicate it across the country. National television coverage was almost unheard of for the women's game.

Then there was the purse. The year the Colgate Dinah Shore debuted in 1972, there were twenty-nine other official LPGA events. Of those, only six had purses of more than $30,000. The largest was the $85,000 at the Sears Women's World Classic in Port St. Lucie, Florida.

So when the Colgate Dinah Shore announced a purse of $110,000, it was a major shockwave for the tour. The $20,050 first-place check was more than the entire purse of six other tournaments. Foster had thought that the big purse would energize the women's game, but in later years, he admitted that he and the LPGA had been surprised when some sponsors of LPGA events simply left the tour, apparently not wanting the pressure of trying

When the Colgate Dinah Shore debuted in 1972, its $110,000 purse was more than any other event on the LPGA Tour. That made it a big deal for winner Jane Blalock. *Courtesy of International Management Group.*

to increase their own purses in response to what Colgate was doing in the Coachella Valley.

The Colgate Dinah Shore Winner's Circle still needed to find the right course in the desert as a home. With so many great courses, surely

While the Mission Hills course is celebrated by LPGA players, it took several years for the area around the course to build up. Nancy Lopez and her caddie celebrate a made putt in the event's early days. *Courtesy of International Management Group.*

someone would be interested in landing what promised to be the biggest women's tournament in the world. But most courses turned the women's event down flat. Max Genet, the president of Mission Hills Country Club, loved to tell the story of how a few courses in the desert suggested that it might be OK to host a women's event, assuming the LPGA players would agree to tee off after the men membership at the club had their morning tee times.

The tournament eventually found a friend in Genet, who was looking for something to give his Mission Hills club an identity. The course was still young, and the eucalyptus trees that would years later tower over the course were still just saplings. With no protection from the harsh desert winds and with undeveloped areas to the west of the course, sand storms became a part of the character of the Colgate Dinah Shore.

The first tournament featured a limited field of forty players for fifty-four holes over the course. And it faced some of the same issues that women's golf had always faced. The lead paragraph in the advance story on the event by the local *Desert Sun* newspaper declared, "The richest girly golf tournament of all time swings into high gear Friday at Mission Hills Country Club."

Jane Blalock, a four-year pro with three wins to her credit, won the event with a score of 3-under 213, 3 shots better than Carol Mann and Judy Rankin. For three days' work in the desert, Blalock earned the $20,050 first-place check, more than half of the $34,492 she won in 1971 with two wins and four second-place finishes.

The 1973 tournament produced both a popular and a historic win. Mickey Wright was now thirty-eight years old and nearing the end of her

Jo Ann Prentice (second from right) won the 1974 Colgate Dinah Shore in a playoff that included 1972 winner Jane Blalock (far left). *Courtesy of International Management Group.*

career. She hadn't won an official event since the 1969 Bluegrass Invitational and was playing less than a full schedule. But with the purse already raised to $135,000 and with the tournament now four rounds instead of three, Wright put together a fabulous win. She managed 4-under 284 for the week while wearing tennis shoes to aid her aching feet. That was two shots better than Joyce Kazmierski. Wright, who was already a fast friend of Shore's, earned $25,000 in what turned out to be the final win of her LPGA career. It was one of only eight events Wright played that year, and she never again played more than eleven times in a season.

Wright kicked off a run in the tournament that featured a who's who of LPGA golfers winning the event, many on their way to the LPGA Hall of Fame. Jo Ann Prentice won in 1974 in a playoff with Jane Blalock and Sandra Haynie. Sandra Palmer and Judy Rankin, a future Hall of Famer, won in 1975 and 1976, respectively, with Rankin winning on what was, at the time, her home course. Then Kathy Whitworth won in 1977, posting a winning score of 1-over 289 in difficult conditions. Whitworth was also a great friend of Shore. Whitworth is fond of telling the story of how Wright and Whitworth were invited to play in Liberty Mutual's Legends of Golf

Even in its early days, the walk to the eighteenth hole at Mission Hills Country Club was special for members of the LPGA. All-time LPGA winner Kathy Whitworth, who won the tournament in 1977, crosses the bridge to the island green. *Courtesy of International Management Group.*

in Texas, the tournament that spawned the men's Champions Tour. Before the tournament, Wright and Whitworth received a telegram from Dinah Shore wishing them good luck and telling the golfers how proud Shore was of them. So important was Shore to even two such veteran stars as Wright and Whitworth that Whitworth turned to Wright and said, "Mickey, I guess we're going to have to arm wrestle over who keeps this telegram."

David Foster had so wanted his women's tournament to be compared to the men's Masters that he wanted to assure that the tournament would remain on one golf course, just as the Masters had Augusta National in Georgia. What better way to secure that than having Colgate-Palmolive buy Mission Hills Country Club? That's what Foster did, closing the deal in January 1975. His own home on the course would be overlooking a lake on the par-4 sixth hole.

Flush with success from the Colgate Dinah Shore, Foster expanded his reach into women's golf. True to his marketing beliefs, Foster had as many as thirty LPGA players doing television commercials for his products, from toothpaste to laundry detergent to dishwashing soap.

"He structured a deal where Jan Stephenson and I, he had a deal where Anne Kline and the company would make a line of sports clothing for women, and Jan Stephenson and I were modeling for it," Marlene Hagge recalled.

Foster also started other tournaments. In 1974, he started the Colgate European Women's Championship played at Sunningdale Golf Club in England and the Colgate Far East Women's Championship. That event would be played in Australia, Singapore, the Philippines and Malaysia. For good measure, Foster and the LPGA devised a points system within the three Colgate events, and the top players in points gathered for the Colgate Triple Crown, played at Mission Hills in December 1975 and January 1977 as a stroke-play event (Jane Blalock won both times) and as a match-play event in 1978 and 1979 (Joanne Carner won both times).

Foster had been named chairman of Colgate-Palmolive in 1975, but he retired in 1979. Perhaps it was because he turned sixty-nine that year. Perhaps it was because others at Colgate-Palmolive were starting to question just how much money the company was putting into women's sports in general, particularly women's golf. It is not a coincidence that Colgate's interest in women's golf began to wane about the same time. By 1982, Colgate was pretty much out of the LPGA all together, and the Coachella Valley's big event was now being run by RJR Nabisco and its charismatic head, Ross Johnson. In 1983, the tournament was designated a major

The golfers in desert tournaments were often not as famous as their pro-am partners. Sally Little, who won the Colgate Dinah Shore in 1981, is seen here with former president Gerald Ford. *Courtesy of International Management Group.*

championship, part of the deal Nabisco had struck with the LPGA in return for its sponsorship. The event was already a major in the eyes of the players, Hagge said.

"Most of the girls would tell you that they would rather have won the Dinah than the U.S. Open," Hagge said. "That's how big that tournament was and how important it was to us."

The 1983 event, the first played as a major, also brought a winner to the tournament who would create history of her own. Like Marlene Hagge and Mickey Wright before her, Amy Alcott was a talented Southern California teenager in golf in a time when opportunities for women in the game were slim. She had won the U.S. Junior Girls Championship in 1973, when she was sixteen, just as Hagge and Wright had done as teenagers.

Nabisco always made sure to bring famous athletes from other sports to its LPGA tournament in the desert. Here, future LPGA Hall of Famer Patty Sheehan watches a shot with baseball legend Joe DiMaggio. *Courtesy of International Management Group.*

Ross Johnson, the head of RJR Nabisco, lavished money on the tournament, both for the professional portion of the event as well as the two-day pro-am that celebrated RJR Nabisco customers and vendors. *Courtesy of International Management Group.*

Among Dinah Shore's friends on the LPGA were LPGA founder and Hall of Famer Marlene Hagge (left) and Hall of Famer Donna Caponi (center). *Courtesy of International Management Group.*

With chances to play in college limited at best, Alcott turned pro at eighteen in 1975. And she started making LPGA news immediately.

"I was very young when I first played in my first Colgate. I had a unique situation because I went out and won my third tournament as a pro, the Orange Blossom," Alcott said. "So everyone was saying now you have qualified for the Colgate. And of course I had heard about it. It was kind of like the tournament that put women's golf on the map. It was a great vision of David Foster, and it was Dinah Shore and the whole thing."

For Alcott, nineteen by the time she played her first Colgate Dinah Shore, the event was larger than life.

"That event had everything. It had Dinah and the star power of her friends. It had the corporate element of a huge company like Colgate-Palmolive behind women's golf and the vision of David Foster, who really believed in women. He was putting women in commercials, and then he bought Ram Golf Company," Alcott recalled.

The Southern California kid who grew up not far from Hollywood was also star-stuck a bit by the high-profile amateur who played in the event.

"I can remember playing with Jack Albertson and Dale Robertson and Robert Stack. All of Dinah's friends. That event was just huge," she said.

Alcott said there was a change in the tournament when RJR Nabisco took over from Colgate-Palmolive.

"It changed a lot. It became a little more opulent. Nabisco at the time was putting a lot of money into golf and Ross was a very, very nice man," Alcott said. "And he spent a lot of money on the tournament. It kind of took the tournament to the next level. Everything went from Colgate to red and white and a big New York presence. I look at these people as people with great vision. In a way with women's golf I think they were ahead of their time."

When Mission Hills Country Club opened a new course designed by Pete Dye in 1990, they named it in honor of resident and tournament hostess Dinah Shore. Shore cuts the ribbon to the course surrounded by officials of Landmark Land, a golf course development company that owned Mission Hills at the time. *Courtesy of International Management Group.*

In that first year of the event designated as a major, Alcott won the Nabisco Dinah Shore for her third career major championship. But it was her second win at the desert tournament that caused a stir. Alcott survived a stiff challenge from Colleen Walker to win the event by two shots. She then did something no one had expected. The par-5 eighteenth hole on the original course at Mission Hills (later renamed the Dinah Shore Tournament Course) features an island green. Golfers had to walk over a bridge to get from the walkway in front of the grandstands to the green.

When Alcott tapped in for her second Nabisco Dinah Shore win, she was struck by inspiration.

Amy Alcott and her caddie Bill Kurre run toward the lake that surrounded the eighteenth hole after winning the 1988 Nabisco Dinah Shore. Alcott's spur-of-the-moment leap started the tradition of winners making a Champions' Leap into Poppie's Pond. *Courtesy of International Management Group.*

"I think it was really just spontaneous. I looked at Bill [Kurre, her caddie] and he looked at me and I said let's jump in the water," Alcott said. "He said, 'Do you want to?' and I said 'Yes.' I don't even know if I took my glove off."

Hand in hand, the player and the caddie raced into the lake, running in more than jumping. The crowd was first stunned and then thrilled with the celebration. Alcott was happy, for a moment at least.

"The water was very dirty. It was disgusting, really," she said. "I got out of the water and I had bird dung in my bra and on my back. I had a white shirt on. The crowd loved it. We loved it. I had no idea it was going to start this tradition in women's golf."

The tradition started slowly, with no one jumping into the lake again until 1991, when Alcott won her third Shore tournament. This time, the seventy-five-year-old Shore joined Alcott and Kurre in the lake.

Left: When Amy Alcott won her third Nabisco Dinah Shore title in 1991, she jumped into the nearby lake for a second time, but in 1991, Alcott was joined in the lake by tournament hostess Dinah Shore. *Courtesy of International Management Group.*

Below: The famous island green on the eighteenth hole of the Dinah Shore Tournament Course at Mission Hills Country Club, where LPGA major champions leap into Poppie's Pond to celebrate victory. *Courtesy of Graeme Baxter Golf Art.*

"Of course when I won in 1991, which was my last tournament win, my mother had just died," Alcott said. "And Dinah knew how devastated I was. She had met my mother. She said, why don't you go out and win it for her, just one more time."

After Donna Andrews won the 1994 Shore and jumped in the lake, it became expected that each winner would jump in. Some have, some have just toe-danced or waded into the lake. Eventually, after 1999 winner Dottie Pepper fell ill a few weeks after jumping in the lake and half-joking that doctors had taken something green out of her ear, plans were made to section off a portion of the lake into a concrete pond with clean, filtered water. The new area was called Poppie's Pond in honor of longtime tournament director Terry Wilcox, whose grandchildren call him Poppie. It's a safer and cleaner place to continue a tradition.

CHAPTER 8
The Big '80s

By PGA Tour standards, Ernie Vossler was more than a decent player. Joining the tour in 1955 out of the Fort Worth, Texas area, Vossler won three tour events, one each in 1958, 1959 and 1960. But Vossler always had his eye out for what he might want to do after his playing days were through.

"When my dad played the tour, he knew he wasn't going to play very long. One of the things he always did was pay good attention to the surroundings and the opportunities," said Andy Vossler. "He would try to spend a few minutes if he could with the most prominent or best-known golf professional in that area. He believed that golf pros in those days knew what was going on and were connected to the influential people because of their golf clubs. And so as he traveled the country playing the PGA Tour he identified in his mind that there were two places that he could end up. They were Palm Springs, California and Monterey, California."

Vossler became familiar with the Coachella Valley by playing in the Bob Hope Classic nine times from 1960 through 1973. He never had much success in the desert as a player, missing the cut seven of his nine starts in the Hope event. But Vossler would have a different kind of success in the desert in just a few years, thanks to his own vision and that of his business partner, another former tour player named Joe Walser.

What Vossler and Walser did, with help from some friends in the desert and outside the Coachella Valley, was literally reshape the desert. They did this by not just physically moving millions and millions of cubic yards of desert sand to create the kinds of golf courses not seen before in the desert but also refocusing the golf world's attention on the Coachella Valley as a world-class golf destination. And their work led to a revitalization of housing development in the desert as well as golf course construction.

If the 1950s were the golden era of golf course development in the Coachella Valley, then the 1980s were the gold rush. Consider that in the 1950s, the decade that established the desert as a golfing destination for the famous and the powerful, fewer than a dozen golf courses were built in the desert. But in the 1980s, thirty-four golf courses were built.

Those courses ranged from eighteen-hole par-3 residential courses like Oasis Country Club in Palm Desert and nine-hole courses for recreational vehicle owners like Sands RV Resort in Desert Hot Springs to perhaps the crème de la crème of desert courses, the Mountain and Desert Courses at the Vintage Club in Indian Wells.

But the fuse that was the explosion of golf courses in the desert in the 1980s was lit a few years earlier, said another man responsible for much of the golf development in the desert, Bill Bone.

"The whole phenomenon started in the '70s and I'm the one who started it," said Bone, whose Sunrise Company did for the 1970s what Johnny Dawson's development eye had done for the 1950s. "It changed things dramatically and it just exploded in the 1980s. But the foundation was laid in 1973."

Bone was already a successful home builder in the early 1970s, with work from northern California to Southern California to Arizona to Las Vegas. But in the Coachella Valley, Bone said development in the 1960s was "as flat as a dead man's EKG." Bone helped to change that with small developments in the 1970s. He was building condominium developments that were springing up through the Palm Springs area.

"They were all built around swimming pools and a few tennis courts," Bone said. "They were gated communities and things like that, but there was no golf course. We were selling the heck out of them."

People took notice of Bone's success, including the folks at Marrakesh Country Club in Palm Desert, an executive course developed by Johnny Dawson. The Marrakesh development was struggling a bit, selling, as Bone recalls, about thirty housing units a year. The Marrakesh team asked Bone to take a look at the development.

"I just looked at Johnny Dawson's plan, I ran the numbers on it and I said, wow, we were making a lot of money selling a lot of houses. If we could do this on a golf course we could even sell more," Bone said.

Bone admits he met resistance within his own company. Company officials thought Bone was crazy, that it was too expensive to build a golf course, that he would have to buy pieces of land that were too big to make economic sense.

"They gave me every reason in the world why it was a bad idea," Bone said. "And I said, well, you know what, I am in charge, it's my money and we are going to do it."

It was a simple plan, really a throwback to Dawson's days at Thunderbird Country Club. Dawson built a course that people could play with plans to sell home lots. Bone's idea was to build the homes himself and sell those to the golfers.

The experiment was at Sunrise Country Club in Rancho Mirage. Bone admits he knew nothing about developing a golf course, but he did know a course architect named Ted Robinson. Bone and Robinson had worked on a project in northern California, which was never built. Bone felt Robinson could give him the kind of course that would complement Bone's condominiums, which were perfect for retired couples and Los Angeles–area residents looking for a weekend getaway home.

Bone had been able to piece together property owned by a variety of men, including Leonard Firestone and Phil Harris. Sunrise Country Club was built in 1973 and ready for business in 1974. And what business it was.

"The opening weekend at Sunrise Country Club we sold 225 houses in two days. I said, whoa, I was dead right," Bone said. "People came out of the woodwork. We built, sold and closed that, there were 749 homes in that community, and we sold it out in three years. I said, man, this is the business to be in."

Bone didn't know how right he was. With Sunrise Country Club as a template, Bone's company quickly developed courses like Rancho Las Palmas Country Club, Monterey Country Club and the Lakes Country Club. Robinson was fast becoming the desert's busiest course designer, eventually designing or renovating two dozen courses. The courses were never going to be considered for the Bob Hope Classic, but the golf, the weather and the growing desert lifestyle of shopping and dining were combining to attracted buyers for Bone's homes. Other developers were starting to copy Bone's plan, perhaps without as much success but still enough to have more and more courses built. But as the 1970s ended, two old PGA Tour pros were about to teach Bone and the other developers in the desert a few lessons.

Ernie Vossler and Joe Walser had developed golf courses in Oklahoma and North Carolina before they started developing in California. They had each bought condos at Del Safari Country Club in Palm Desert to use as a

This aerial view of the city of La Quinta in late 1986 or early 1987 shows the impact of golf in the desert. Two courses at PGA West can clearly be seen in the middle left of the photo, the Palmer Private Course closest to the mountain and the TPC Stadium Course below the Palmer Course. In the center right is a complex that includes La Quinta Resort's two courses and La Quinta Country Club. *Courtesy of La Quinta Historical Society.*

La Quinta Country Club's clubhouse, with the ninth green of the course in the foreground. *Courtesy of Graeme Baxter Golf Art.*

base, and they were on the lookout for the right chance. According to Andy Vossler, it was Ernie's and Joe's wives who one day decided to drive up a little road to La Quinta Hotel, just to check out what it was. They insisted that their husbands take a look at the property. Joe and Ernie liked what they saw, plenty of undeveloped land around an established hotel in a cove protected from the desert winds by mountains.

About the same time, Vossler and Walser heard that the folks at La Quinta Country Club were about to end their longtime policy of letting hotel guests use the country club course during their stays. Vossler sought out Leonard Ettleson, who also owned the hotel, and they began a relationship centered on what was best for the La Quinta Hotel property. Eventually, Vossler and Walser convinced Ettleson to sell them the land around the hotel, and Vossler and Walser's vision began to take shape.

"They really made a great team," said Marlene Hagge, who would eventually marry Vossler. "Ernie had all of these ideas. He was the let's go, go, go guy. Joe was the guy who would say, now, pro, let's think about this a minute. Is this what we want to do? They really helped each other."

Before any land could be developed at all at La Quinta Hotel—or, as it turned out, many parts of the growing community of La Quinta—a major issue had to be attacked. Much of La Quinta was nothing but a flood plain at the base of the Santa Rosa Mountains. Without a flood control plan, and money to pay for it, water from the south end of the city would flow through any residential areas, including the one that Vossler and Walser planned for the Santa Rosa Cove at La Quinta Hotel.

"The flood control work and the golf course construction coincided in time. But we got to see water at one time come right through the lobby of La Quinta Hotel," Andy Vossler said. "It wasn't more than two or three inches thick. It was more foam and mud than it was water. But it was damaging and it was a mess and that had to be deal with."

Future courses like Rancho La Quinta Country Club and Tradition Golf Club owe their existences to that flood control work in the early 1980s. But with the flooding issue addressed, another issue was who was going to come in and design the two courses Joe and Ernie had planned. The answer turned out to be a very good amateur golfer and former insurance salesman from Indiana.

"When my dad and Joe had made their mind up they were going to get into golf and real estate development, they traveled the country and talked to several people," Andy Vossler said. "One of the ones they had a lot of confidence in, I shouldn't say one, was Jackie Burke and Jimmy Demaret. They spent quite a bit of time in Houston talking to them. They had a lot of confidence in [PGA Tour commissioner] Deane Beman's opinions."

The name that kept coming up in the discussions was Pete Dye. Dye and Vossler and Walser first worked together on a course called the Cardinal in North Carolina. Dye came to the desert to team up again with Vossler and Walser, who by now were working for a company called Landmark Land. Dye designed the Dunes Course and the Mountain Course for La Quinta Hotel, two spectacular courses at the base of the Santa Rosa Mountains. But Dye's most famous, or infamous, design for the desert was still a few years away.

South and east of La Quinta Hotel was more developable land. Andy Vossler recalls driving through the property with the president of Landmark Land, Gerald Barton.

"I was driving down through there and we were going through that farm land and it was all planted and in crops and Gerry said. 'You know, this is where it is going to happen next. This will be the next area of development. What do you all know about this property.' And I told him not a lot," Andy Vossler said.

A little research and a little money later, and Landmark Land had the property that would become the largest golf development the desert had ever seen, PGA West. And, according to Bill Bone, Landmark almost didn't get the property.

"I actually had a deal to buy all of the PGA West land," Bone said. "I shook hands with the owners. I said I am going on a week's vacation, drop the contract by, I will sign it when I get back. I came back, where is the contract? Well, Ernie and Joe had already tied the thing up in the week I was gone."

Even though Vossler and Walser had built homes before in developments in Louisiana, the scales of PGA West made them think about bringing in a home developer with success in the desert. That's why they called Bone and asked for a meeting. Bone's first suggestion was to wait five or ten years until civilization developed closer to PGA West, some ten miles from the main artery of Highway 111.

"It was too risky. I didn't think you could do the volume. With that much money you can't just do 50 or 60 or 75 [homes] a year. It doesn't work. They said, well, we're going anyway, and I said, well, okay, count me in," Bone said. "The first year we opened we sold something like 400 houses out there. Are you kidding me, out in the middle of nowhere? The streets are hardly paved."

Bone had worked at his courses with Ted Robinson and other good but low-profile course designers. Vossler and Walser had other plans. That included getting Pete Dye to do the first course at PGA West. Vossler and Dye had just one demand of Dye: build the toughest damn course in America. Most recreational golfers at the time would say Dye exceeded expectations with the TPC Stadium Course, a monster of a course at over 7,400 yards from the back tees, with twenty-foot-deep bunkers, 200-yard forced carries over water, a moat bunker around one green and a famous island green on the par-3 seventeenth known as Alcatraz.

"I said to Ernie, why do we want to do that? My homeowners typically aren't very good golfers. Why would you want to do that?" Bone said. "He said, oh now, we are going to build them for everybody. We are going to have the Palmer course and the Nicklaus course. We are going to do this and that. I said okay, guys, you think this is a good idea. But I am telling you, the people I am selling homes to, they are not going to be real thrilled if you make that the toughest golf course."

Vossler and Walser proved to be geniuses. The publicity from the TPC Stadium Course brought more attention to PGA West. People started flocking to the course to play the toughest course in the country. Bone had learned a lesson. A top designer did add value to a property.

How can you tell Pete Dye was the architect of the TPC Stadium Course at PGA West in La Quinta? By his characteristic use of railroad ties, a Dye trademark. *Courtesy of La Quinta Historical Society.*

"They brought in the Palmers and the Nicklauses and the Pete Dyes, who had never really existed in the desert before. And Mick Humphreys did The Vintage Club, and that was in [the] 1980s, and that was Tom Fazio's first effort here in the desert," Bone said. "So all of a sudden, people got exposed to world class golf. I have not built another Ted Robinson–style resort type since then. Everything we had done since then has been either with Palmer or Nicklaus or Dye or people like that. Ernie and Joe taught me that."

Even today, Dye's TPC Stadium Course is a cause for debate. On the course's twentieth anniversary, Dye attended a gala celebration at PGA West. One by one, members would walk up to Dye, thank him for coming, shake his hand and tell him how much they hated his golf course. Dye would just laugh.

Inscribed in the lobby of the clubhouse that serves the Stadium Course are these words from Dye.

"Thanks to Ernie Vossler and Joe Walser, I had the opportunity to design and build The Stadium Course. Love and Hate can be found here."

Few holes in the desert are as famous or picturesque as the par-3 seventeenth on the TPC Stadium Course at PGA West in La Quinta, known as Alcatraz. *Courtesy of Graeme Baxter Golf Art.*

Vossler and Walser also understood the appeal of professional golfers, touring pros, for the average recreational player. They put together a team of golfers called the Oak Tree Gang, golfers who would wear the company logo of an oak tree wherever and whenever they played golf. That team included names like Fred Couples, John Cook, Gil Morgan, Willie Wood and Bob Tway. Vossler and Walser were trying to build value in any way they could.

The name PGA West was not a reference to the PGA Tour, although Joe and Ernie had a great relationship with the tour and commissioner Deane Beman. Instead, it was a deal that Landmark Land did with the PGA of America that produced the name. The PGA of America already had PGA National in Florida, and the idea was to do the same thing for the West Coast.

"We paid $1,000 for every home we sold, I think split between the PGA of America and the tour, for the rights to the name," Andy Vossler said. At one time, the PGA of America was so interested in what Vossler and Walser were doing that it was working on a plan to have a West Coast headquarters just a block from PGA West.

If the property needed any more publicity, it came in the form of the Skins Game on Thanksgiving weekend in 1986, with Arnold Palmer, Jack Nicklaus, Lee Trevino and Fuzzy Zoeller, nine holes on Saturday and nine holes on Sunday broadcast to the country on NBC. With the rest of the country cold or under snow, the bright La Quinta sunshine, the high-profile foursome and Dye's masterpiece had the country talking about PGA West.

Two months later, the course was played for the first time in the Bob Hope Classic. It was also the last time for Dye's course in the Classic. In 1987, TPC-style courses were unheard of on the tour. The Stadium Course was still young, and its greens needed more time to mature. The weather was cold and a bit windy that week. The Stadium Course ate up many of the pros. And the pros fired back. Ken Green said there was nothing wrong with the course a few sticks of dynamite wouldn't fix. Tip O'Neill never did figure out how to get his golf ball out of the twenty-foot-deep bunker on the sixteenth hole, flailing away on national television. Curtis Strange said his mother had taught him that if he didn't have anything nice to say, say nothing at all. He said nothing.

Within a week of the end of that 1987 Hope, won by Corey Pavin, rumor was that there was a petition in the locker room of the Los Angeles Open

Bighorn sheep are a familiar sight at desert golf courses near the mountains at dawn and near dusk as they come down to feed, as they are doing here on the Palmer Private Course at PGA West. *Courtesy of Graeme Baxter Golf Art.*

demanding the TPC Stadium Course be taken out of the Hope rotation. The truth was tournament officials had already had a meeting, deciding to dump the Stadium Course for the new Arnold Palmer Course at PGA West because of complaints from pros and amateurs. But the controversy brought more and more attention to PGA West, just as Joe and Ernie had hoped.

After the Palmer Course was built, Vossler and Walser went to Jack Nicklaus for the next design. Andy Vossler says Nicklaus turned the offer down cold. But a good friend of Jack and Barbara Nicklaus was a woman named Katy Gardner who worked for Landmark Land in membership sales.

"One of the things that came out of Katy talking to Jack was that why did they start with Pete? Why was Arnold second? And I think that was Jack's intelligence of negotiating because when it all got done, he said, okay, I'll come to PGA West if I can build two courses," Andy Vossler said. "So it was his way of one-upping them, doing two courses."

It all seemed like it could go on forever. But within just a few years of the opening of the first four courses at PGA West, it all came crashing down for Landmark Land, Vossler and Walser. Landmark Land had, at the urging of the federal government, opened a saving and loan in Louisiana

The short par-3 seventeenth hole on the Palmer Private Course at PGA West offers danger from the Coachella Branch of the All-American Canal to the left and the rugged Santa Rosa Mountains to the right. *Courtesy of Graeme Baxter Golf Art.*

"Gerry Barton, in leading our board in a direction, was able to influence them to buy three more S and Ls. And when the government decided to change the rules on everybody, there was no way out for us," Andy Vossler said.

The government foreclosed on the Landmark S and Ls, and since those S and Ls held the resort properties and golf courses, those properties were seized, too. Landmark had filed for bankruptcy, but the properties were all auctioned off. By the time Landmark's lawsuit won in court and awarded the company and its officers $20 million, the golf courses were gone to other owners. In the Coachella Valley, that included PGA West, La Quinta Hotel and Mission Hills Country Club, which Landmark had bought and for which it had even developed a third course, designed by Pete Dye.

Vossler and Walser tried to continue development with a new company, Landmark Golf, and did develop courses in Southern California and the Coachella Valley. But they never had the great success they had at La Quinta Hotel and PGA West again. Andy Vossler isn't sure that kind of success will be seen again.

"I might not live long enough to see it and if I had to guess where it will be, it will be closely related to the high tech industry," Vossler said. "But when things get to running at a pitch that accelerates history, you better watch out."

CHAPTER 9
Tournaments, Tournaments and More Tournaments

Lee Trevino's shot from the elevated tee flew high in the air and right at the target.

"That's a pretty shot," said Trevino's playing partner, Jack Nicklaus.

Seconds later, the ball Trevino had launched with a 6-iron landed on the island green of the par-3 seventeenth hole on the TPC Stadium Course, took one hop and rolled gently into the cup 167 yards from the tee. The crowd, estimated at anywhere from eight to fifteen thousand, depending on who was doing the estimating, went crazy.

The Skins Game was in its fifth year in 1987 and just its second at PGA West in the Coachella Valley. But Trevino's hole in one worth $175,000 had paid off the promise of the big-money format. A single shot could be worth hundreds of thousands of dollars in the event where there was no crystal trophy, just a giant check. Taped in the morning at PGA West on the Sunday after Thanksgiving, Trevino's ace in the brilliant sunshine of the desert and his celebratory leap into the arms of caddy Herman Mitchell were beamed across the country that afternoon on NBC. The Skins Game had a magical moment, and so did the TPC Stadium Course, PGA West and desert golf.

The Skins Game did more than just give the Coachella Valley another highly rated televised golf event, showing off the desert, its environment and its sunshine to the country on a cold Thanksgiving weekend. Conceived by Emmy-winning television sports producer Don Ohlmeyer and executed by Ohlmeyer and television executive Barry Frank, the Skins Game fundamentally changed the nature of professional golf. In the 1970s and into the 1980s, the PGA Tour had a very definite off-season. In 1982, the tour ended its schedule on October 31 at the Walt Disney World Golf Classic in Florida. That was the last tour event until January 6, 1983, at the Joe Garagiola Tucson Open.

Ohlmeyer and Frank figured that, with the right format and more importantly the right players, they could fill a winter void for golf-starved fans. Let the players show off their personalities more than they could in a regular PGA Tour event. Give those players a chance to make timely shots for huge money.

"On a scale of what is more important, first is the players, second is the concept, the money and then the site," Frank said on the twenty-fifth anniversary of the Skins Game in 2008.

The first Skins Game was played over Thanksgiving weekend at Desert Highlands Country Club in Scottsdale, Arizona, in 1983 with a lineup of some of the biggest names to ever play the game. Jack Nicklaus, Arnold Palmer, Tom Watson and Gary Player made up the foursome playing one of the oldest games in golf. The origin of the term "skins" has been debated for years, but the game basically gives the outright winner of the hole a designated amount of money. If no one wins a hole outright, the money for that hole carries over to the next hole. In the 1983 Skins Game, the total prize money for the four players was $360,000. The purse for a field of 128 pros in the 1983 Bob Hope Classic had been just $408,000.

In that first Skins Game, Arnold Palmer made a $100,000 putt, Gary Player won the event with $170,000 and the rating for NBC proved Ohlmeyer had been right all along. The Skins Game had the same ratings as the British Open, one of men's golf's four majors. In 1984 and 1985, the event had more viewers than the U.S. Open, the PGA Championship and the British Open.

After two years at Desert Highlands and one year at Bear Creek Golf Club in Murrieta, California, the Skins Game moved to Pete Dye's beast of a golf course, the TPC Stadium Course at PGA West in La Quinta. The players were Palmer, Nicklaus, Trevino and Zoeller, but the event now had a fifth star in the torturous and dramatic Stadium Course. Vin Scully's fabulous voice opened the NBC telecast with the words, "It. Is. Awesome." No one could argue the point.

Zoeller won the 1986 event in front of a massive gallery that scrambled over the spectator mounds and through the native desert plants craning for a view of four guys playing the same hole. When the ratings came out early the next week, the news was stunning. The Skins Game had outdrawn all four of the major championships, even the venerable Masters that annually ruled television ratings in golf.

The Skins Game was proving another point that PGA West developer Ernie Vossler and Joe Walser had always believed. Television was a great way to market your golf course development.

"Most golf course developers didn't really appreciate the value and technique of tournament golf for real estate. They just didn't quite understand that," said Andy Vossler. "The second thing is in those earliest years, the competition didn't know how to go get a PGA Tour tournament. Joe and Ernie had done that for Quail Creek in Oklahoma City in the early '60s."

The Skins Game was bringing worldwide attention to PGA West even before Trevino's ace. It was helping to sell homes at the La Quinta development and in the desert as much as the two other big established tournaments in the desert, the Bob Hope Classic and the Nabisco Dinah Shore. But those three events were just part of an unprecedented cavalry charge of professional golf events in the Coachella Valley in the 1980s and 1990s, many inspired directly by the success of the Skins Game.

There was one tournament that predated the Skins Game in the 1980s, and it was at the forefront of a new concept of tournaments for players fifty and older. The Champions Tour, then known as the Senior PGA Tour, didn't officially exist until 1980, even though the tournament that inspired the fifty-and-over circuit was first played in 1978. That was the Liberty Mutual's Legends of Golf, won by the team of Sam Snead and Gardner Dickinson when Snead birdied the final three holes of the final round. In 1979, again with NBC televising, Roberto De Vicenzo and Julius Boros won an epic six-hole playoff over Tommy Bolt and Art Wall, and everyone knew senior golf was going to have a place in the golf world. The following year, the Senior PGA Tour became official, with just two tournaments.

At about the same time, developers Mick Humphreys and Jay Seiger were working a 712-acre piece of land at the base of the Santa Rosa Mountains in India Wells, just west of Eldorado Country Club. It was to be called the Vintage Club and eventually feature two golf courses by a young designer named Tom Fazio and his uncle, a talented former PGA Tour player and Pennsylvania club professional named George Fazio. Tom Fazio was building up a résumé of excellent courses, but they were all on the East Coast—Florida, the Carolinas, sometimes up to New Jersey and even into Canada. Humphreys, a friend of Fazio, convinced the young architect to come to California to build Humphreys's two courses. The first course opened in 1980 with nearby Eisenhower Mountain as backdrop. It was known as the Mountain Course, since it ran right up the edge of the Santa Rosa Mountains. Fazio would later design the Desert Course, a layout away from the mountains.

The Vintage Club quickly established itself as perhaps the finest high-end private club in the desert, with high-profile and powerful members from corporate America and with the club featuring the finest in facilities. It was on the Mountain Course, which had also quickly been recognized as one of the best courses in the desert, where Humphreys decided to play a senior golf event. Thirty select competitors played in the first event from March 12 to 15, 1981, preceded by a pro-am. Featured in the pro-am was Bob Hope, who was friends with so many of the older golfers. The field ranged from legends like Sam Snead, Paul Runyan and Gene Sarazen to international players like Bobby Locke, Peter Thomson and Kel Nagle and stars who had just recently turn fifty like Arnold Palmer and Gene Littler.

The first Vintage event was not considered an official Senior PGA Tour stop, but that didn't stop organizers from having grand plans.

"The Vintage Club has dedicated this tournament to be an event which emphasizes the tradition of golf. We invited a special field and next year with our new clubhouse will have the facilities for [a] larger crowd," Humphreys said at the first event in 1981.

The appeal of the senior circuit was immediate, at least for the golfers.

"Here you can get back together with the people you traveled with for 20 years and you talk a lot, tell a lot of stories, tell a lot of lies and have a lot of fun," early Senior PGA Tour star Don January said at the Vintage event.

Sam Snead, sixty-eight at the time, led the inaugural tournament for two rounds, but Gene Littler, who had won amateur events in the desert in the 1950s, ran away on the weekend with rounds of 65 and 64 to win by 9 shots over Bob Goalby. Littler earned $50,000 from a $300,000 purse. By the time the second event was played in 1982, there was already talk of the Vintage Invitational being a kind of Masters for the Senior PGA Tour. Miller Barber won the title in 1982, Littler won again in 1983 and, by 1984, the event had earned designation as an official Senior PGA Tour event when Don January won.

There was no questioning now that the Coachella Valley was as important a center for professional golf as anywhere in the country. The desert had the Bob Hope Classic on the PGA Tour, a major championship in the Nabisco Dinah Shore on the LPGA Tour, the elegant Vintage Invitational on the Senior PGA Tour and the raucous and fun-loving Skins Game in the off-season. By 1984, Ernie Vossler and Joe Walser and their connections to the

In 1984, an LPGA rookie named Juli Inskter won the Nabisco Dinah Shore title and would go on to win the title again in 1989 on her way to the LPGA Hall of Fame. *Courtesy of International Management Group.*

PGA Tour had lured the six-day PGA Tour qualifying finals, or Q-school for short, to the desert to be played every other year or so on Landmark Land courses at PGA West, La Quinta Hotel and Mission Hills Country Club.

With such success, it was inevitable that more tournaments would want to come to the desert. The Skins Game had shown that desert sunshine, star golfers and different formats could draw a television audience in the PGA Tour's off-season. The Skins Game had also shown that it could be used as a device to sell real estate. As Landmark Land was preparing to fight its financial battles with the federal government in the early 1990s, the Skins Game moved to a development in the foothills of south Palm Desert called Bighorn Golf Club. The big crowds that had followed the Skins foursome weren't on the Mountain Course at Bighorn, with galleries limited by the rocky up-and-down terrain of Arthur Hills's design for the Mountain Course. With original Skins Game stars like Arnold Palmer, Jack Nicklaus and Lee Trevino fading away or playing in a senior version of the event in Hawaii, new names like Payne Stewart, Fred Couples, Paul Azinger and Corey Pavin were now playing. Television ratings dropped a bit but remained strong as Stewart won three straight Skins Games from 1991 to 1993. In the first three events at Bighorn, Fred Couples finished second each year and then won the event in 1995. It was the first of five Skins Games wins for Couples, who seemed to capitalize on the Skins format by not playing well for eighteen holes each year, but playing well at the moment when the most money was at stake. With other wins in the Shark Shootout, Couples would earn the title of the King of the Silly Season.

Bighorn sold plenty of real estate during its four-year run with the Skins Game, and the event would move to another new emerging development, Rancho La Quinta Country Club, in 1996. Naturally, Fred Couples won that year, but the event also featured a new star playing in the desert for the first time as a professional. Tiger Woods was no stranger to the Coachella Valley, having won two American Junior Golf Association events at Mission Hills Country Club and one California Interscholastic Federation Southern Section high school title at Canyon Country Club in Palm Springs. He would eventually play in the Skins Game five times but never won the title. And he never played in the Bob Hope Classic, with rumors of bad blood between the Woods camp and tournament officials seeming to play as much a part in Woods staying away as a potential dislike of the event's five-day, four-course pro-am format or the short, tight desert layouts.

By the time Woods played in his first Skins Game, two other so-called Silly Season tournaments had already made their debuts in the Coachella

Valley on courses once owned by Landmark Land that were bought by a development company called KSL. The first was the intriguing Diners Club Matches, which began in December 1994 on the Jack Nicklaus Resort Course at PGA West in La Quinta. It was actually three tournaments in one, with a simple team match-play format but with a PGA Tour, a Senior PGA Tour and an LPGA division. Tammie Green and Kelly Robbins won the LPGA division the first year, with Jeff Maggert and Jim McGovern winning the PGA Tour division. The drama was in the Senior PGA Tour division, where Jack Nicklaus and Arnold Palmer teamed up much as they had in the old Canada Cup Matches and in Ryder Cups. Large crowds gathered every day as the Nicklaus-Palmer team worked its way into the finals against Raymond Floyd and Dave Eichelberger. Surely Nicklaus and Palmer would polish off the popular victory and give the Diners Club matches a signature moment.

But leading 1-up on the final hole, Palmer, Nicklaus and the crowd were stunned when Eichelberger rolled in a long birdie putt to halve the hole and deny the King and the Bear. Floyd and Eichelberger then won the match and the title on the first playoff hole. It was one of the least popular victories in desert golf history. The Grinch had stolen Christmas from the gallery.

Floyd was instrumental in the next Silly Season event in the desert, the Lexus Challenge. Debuting in 1995 at the Citrus Course at La Quinta Hotel the Lexus Challenge was Floyd's idea of re-creating what had been the best parts of the old Crosby Clambake in Pebble Beach or the years of the popular midweek Jam Session that had been an integral part of the fun at the Bob Hope Classic. The event would pair twelve Senior PGA Tour players with twelve celebrities for a team match-play format, with the celebrities using their handicaps.

Plagued in its first year by last-minute cancellations by celebrities, the tournament still survived to feature not only senior professionals like Floyd, Arnold Palmer, Lee Trevino, Johnny Miller, Chi Chi Rodriguez and others but also celebrities like Sean Connery, Kevin Costner, Glenn Frey, Matthew McConaughey, Chis O'Donnell, Clint Eastwood and William Devane. Floyd won his own tournament twice, in 1995 with actor Michael Chiklis and in 1997 with actor William Devane.

With all of that golf, there was still occasionally room for a little more. The Senior Skins Game was played in the desert in 1989 at the Mountain Course at La Quinta Hotel, with Chi Chi Rodriguez winning. After being chased out of two dates in two locations by bad weather, the Wendy's Three-Tour Challenge was played on the PGA West Nicklaus Resort Course in

1994. Because of weather damage to golf courses in Hawaii, the PGA of America's four-player Grand Slam of Golf was played on the Nicklaus Resort Course in 1992 and 1993.

In 1995, with the Vintage Invitational gone since 1993 (first voted off the Vintage Club by members and then ended after one year of play at the Indian Wells Golf Resort), the desert became home to the original Senior PGA Tour event, the Liberty Mutual's Legends of Golf. It was played on the formidable TPC Stadium Course in 1995 and 1996 and then switched to the Palmer Course at PGA West in 1997.

It was a dizzying array of professional events, and no area in the country could claim to match to Coachella Valley for tournaments and high-profile players. In the mid-1990s, the 120 or so days between Thanksgiving and the end of March saw the desert as home to six nationally televised tournaments, three official events on their respective tours and three in the Silly Season.

But perhaps it was getting to be too much, even for the golf-crazed Coachella Valley that was seeing the number of courses in the area creep toward one hundred. The tournaments found themselves fighting for galleries and, perhaps as importantly, volunteers. With guaranteed money in the Silly Season events in November and December, all spawned by the success of the Skins Game, some PGA Tour players were skipping January and February official tour events, including the Bob Hope Classic. Even Fred Couples, the Skins Game king and the 1998 Bob Hope winner, was wondering if enough was enough.

"You played 20 or 25 PGA events, then five or six [postseason events]—that can be a lot of golf," Couples said at the 1995 Bob Hope tournament, the same year he won the Skins Game and three years before his Hope victory.

Even PGA Tour commissioner Tim Finchem was taking notice, and he wanted to ensure that official events like the Bob Hope Classic weren't being damaged by Silly Season events in the desert. Finchem said at Bermuda Dunes Country Club during the 1995 Hope Classic that the desert did seem oversaturated with golf tournaments. So perhaps it is no surprise that some of the events began to disappear, perhaps just a thinning of the herd for the desert.

Terry Jastrow, producer of the Diners Club Matches, was never satisfied with the galleries his event drew in the desert, and the event left after the 1997 matches, to be transformed into the short-lived Hyundai Team Matches. The Legends of Golf suffered from tee times so early (6:30 a.m.) to make live television on the East Coast that few fans were on hand, even for legends like Arnold Palmer. And something never seemed quite right about having Hall of Famers like Snead playing such a modern golf course as the TPC Stadium. After the 1997 tournament, the Legends of Golf headed to Florida.

When Lexus pulled its sponsorship of the Ray Floyd Lexus Challenge after four years, Floyd was confident the tournament would find another million-dollar sponsor to keep the event going. But no new sponsor was found, and the Lexus Challenge faded off the Senior PGA Tour schedule after the 1998 event.

As the 1990s ended, the Coachella Valley had seen the tide of professional golf tournaments roll into only an ebb. The desert was down to its Big Three golf tournaments, the Bob Hope Classic, the Nabisco Dinah Shore and the Skins Game. Other changes were happening in the desert golf world in the 1990s, and more were coming in the next decade.

CHAPTER 10

Changes in the Desert

Bob Hope seemed to be a part of the desert golf scene from the time it began. That wasn't actually true, of course, since Hope and his wife, Dolores, didn't even move to California until 1937 as he started his long movie career.

He bought his first home in the desert in the 1940s, was among the first members of the desert's first eighteen-hole course at Thunderbird Country Club in 1951, entertained at Ryder Cup matches in the 1950s and played in just about every desert pro-am he could fit into his busy schedule. Most importantly, he gave desert golf a massive boost by hosting the area's PGA Tour event starting in 1965 and elevating the event to one of the biggest and most popular events on the tour. More than anyone, Bob Hope was the face of golf in the Coachella Valley.

So when Hope died on July 27, 2003, at the age of one hundred, it was natural that the desert and the international golf world felt the loss.

"In addition to his worldwide renown as an entertainer [Hope] was a key figure in the growth of the popularity of golf in America," PGA Tour commissioner Tim Finchem said. "The tournament bearing his name, the Bob Hope Chrysler Classic dates to 1960 and has long been one of the most successful on the PGA Tour. A mixture of golf and entertainment, the tournament over the years has brought presidents, athletes and other celebrities together with PGA Tour professionals to raise millions of dollars for charities in the Palm Springs area."

No matter when or where he showed up to play in the Coachella Valley, Bob Hope always drew a crowd. *Courtesy of Desert Classic Archives.*

Hope had not actually been at his own tournament since 2000, and he hadn't been on the course for a full eighteen holes in the pro-am since the day he played with the three presidents in 1995. But Hope's death showed that many things in the Coachella Valley and golf were changing in the 1990s and 2000s.

Nine years before Hope's death, the LPGA and the desert faced a similar loss. Dinah Shore had hosted the LPGA major at Mission Hills Country Club in Rancho Mirage since the tournament debuted in 1972. She kept the fact that she was battling ovarian cancer extremely quiet, so when she died on February 24, 1994, at seventy-seven, the news came as a shock.

"Not only was she a great ambassador for the LPGA, but for all of golf," said Charles Mechem, who had just taken over as commissioner of the LPGA. "It is very difficult to put into words what she had meant to the LPGA." One month later, at Shore's own tournament, Mechem had the honor of announcing that Shore was to become the first non-player inducted into the LPGA Hall of Fame. It was a deserving honor that came too late for Shore to receive in person.

Inevitably, Shore's name was taken off her tournament for the 2000 event, in part because a younger and more international group of players was coming along who perhaps didn't know much about Dinah Shore other than she was involved with women's golf. By 2012, in another example of time marching on, Bob Hope's name was no longer on his tournament.

The deaths of two desert golf icons certainly didn't usher in change for the desert or their respective tournaments. But it did highlight that things were transitioning to an updated world. That was certainly true on the golf development scene. The 1980s had been a decade of wild development in the desert, averaging one golf course opening every

Tournament host Bob Hope made appearances at his Classic tournament through 2000, just three years before he died at the age of one hundred in 2003. *Courtesy of Desert Classic Archives.*

one hundred days for ten years. Most of those golf courses had either housing developments or resort hotels attached. But in the 1990s, things slowed drastically. But while courses weren't being built at the same pace, the kind of courses that were being built was changing. Instead of courses lined by condos or even larger but standard individual homes, large golf courses with large home lots available for custom-built homes were springing up. In a sense, it was a throwback to what had happened at Thunderbird Country Club in 1951, only with larger home lots for sale and far more expensive homes being built.

The developers of the 1990s were following the path blazed by Ernie Vossler and Joe Walser in the 1980s by bringing only big-name architects to

How do you know you've made it in the Coachella Valley? They name a street after you like they did for Dinah Shore. *Courtesy of International Management Group.*

the area. Tom Fazio, whose courses at the Vintage Club in the 1980s had his only desert designs, was suddenly designing courses like the Canyons Course at Bighorn, the Quarry at La Quinta and the Madison Club.

The par-4 sixteenth hole on the South Course at Ironwood Country Club looks down from the hills of south Palm Desert toward the desert floor. *Courtesy of Graeme Baxter Golf Art.*

The Tom Fazio design at Madison Club in La Quinta has become a hot spot for famous celebrities as well as pros from the PGA Tour looking to sharpen their game in the off-season. *Courtesy of Graeme Baxter Golf Art.*

Desert courses never really lack for water, as seen here on the tenth hole at SilverRock Resort in La Quinta. *Courtesy of Graeme Baxter Golf Art.*

The Santa Rosa Mountains serve as both a backdrop for desert courses as well as a home for some desert holes. Here, the mountains loom over the eighth green at SilverRock Resort in La Quinta. *Courtesy of Graeme Baxter Golf Art.*

Arnold Palmer did two courses for Bill Bone's Sunrise Company at Indian Ridge Country Club and added courses like Tradition Golf Club and Mountain View Country Club in La Quinta, the city-owned SilverRock Resort in La Quinta and Classic Club in Palm Desert.

An old design by Tom Weiskopf and Jay Moorish that had sat on the drawing table for years was finally built at the Reserve Club. Bill Bone also reached out to Jack Nicklaus for two course designs at Toscana Country Club in Indian Wells. Adding to the courses was Clive Clark, a former English touring pro and one-time Ryder Cupper for the Great Britain and Ireland team. A desert resident, Clark built courses for the Indian Wells Golf Resort, Eagle Falls at Fantasy Springs Golf Resort and one of two courses at the Hideaway in La Quinta. The second course at the Hideaway went to Pete Dye, who had been at the forefront of big-name architects at the start of the 1980s.

Real estate was still driving course development in the desert, but with the ups and downs in the real estate market came ups and downs in course development. For Bone, golf was never the one driving force in building his home or even attracting people to the desert.

"Of all the 10,000 plus homes we built in the desert over the last 40 years, over half the people who have bought homes at our golf course communities

The opening hole of the Clive Clark Course at the Hideaway in La Quinta shows Clark's flair for color and landscaping. *Courtesy of Graeme Baxter Golf Art.*

Johnny Miller's wins in the Bob Hope Classic in 1975 and 1976 helped earn him the nickname the Desert Fox in the 1970s. Here, Miller (right) talks with comedian Flip Wilson (left) before teeing off. *Courtesy of Desert Classic Archives.*

were non-golfers. Over half," he said. "Why did they buy there? Why do people come here to the desert? The weather is Number One. Golf is not the big driver of things in the Coachella Valley. We think it is, but it's not.

"The people who come here, they come here for the weather. But they all shop, they all dine out. A few people play golf. But they all like to sit on the patio and look at the golf course, the beauty of the golf course," Bone added. "And they are there for the beauty and the scenery and the environment that has been created. That's why they buy on a golf course, and not just a house on a street in the desert."

The architects weren't the only stars still making news in the desert. Arnold Palmer had been the desert's biggest winner from the 1950s to the 1970s, taking six official PGA Tour events in the desert in fifteen years. Johnny Miller had earned the nickname the Desert Fox for his brilliant play in PGA Tour events in Arizona and the Coachella Valley, including the only back-to-back wins in the Bob Hope Classic in tournament history in 1975 and 1976. Amy Alcott's three wins in eight years made her the desert star of the 1980s, and Betsy King matched those three Kraft wins from 1987 to 1997. But the desert and the golf world found a new dominant star in the 2000s, one who started her golf career as a young star in her native Sweden.

Annika Sorenstam was so shy as a junior golfer that she would find a way to deliberately lose tournaments so she wouldn't have to give a speech when she accepted a trophy. But her talent overcame her shyness, and she eventually played college golf at the University of Arizona, winning an NCAA women's individual title as a freshman. She turned pro in 1992, was rookie of the year on the Ladies European Tour in 1993 and then rookie of the year on the LPGA in 1994.

In 1995, she won the U.S. Women's Open, and then she won the national title again in 1996.

It's difficult to believe now, but from 1997 through 2000, there was a knock on Sorenstam that she couldn't win the big event, even with two U.S. Women's Open titles to her credit. In that 2000 Nabisco Dinah Shore, the news wasn't about Sorenstam as much as it was about a thirteen-year-old amateur named Michelle Wie who finished tied for ninth after playing in the final threesome on Sunday. Karrie Webb won the tournament by a ridiculous ten shots, a tournament record that had people talking about Webb, not Sorenstam, as women's golf's top player.

That all started to change in the Coachella Valley in 2001. A clearly more determined Sorenstam won her third major title and the first at the desert major, now called the Kraft Nabisco Championship. It was part of an eight-

When tournament director Terry Wilcox invited thirteen-year-old Michelle Wie to play in the 2003 Kraft Nabisco Championship, some questioned if she was too young. Wie, here with her father and caddie B.J., finished tied for ninth that year, fourth the next year and one shot out of a playoff in 2006 as a sixteen-year-old. *Courtesy of International Management Group.*

win season that stamped her as the LPGA's best player. In 2002, Sorenstam again won the Kraft, this time by a single shot over her countrywomen and Mission Hills resident Liselotte Neumann. Sorenstam won eleven times in 2002 and was now in the argument for best golfer on the planet, not just in women's golf. She also joined Sandra Post as the only golfers to win at Mission Hills Country Club in consecutive years, Post doing it in 1978 and 1979 before the tournament was officially a major.

Sorenstam was second in 2003 at Mission Hills, missing out on a third consecutive title when she finished a shot behind surprise winner Patricia Meunier-Lebouc of France. But the desert highlight for Annika that year came over Thanksgiving weekend, when she was invited to be the first woman to play in the Skins Game. Facing Fred Couples, Phil Mickelson and Mark O'Meara at Trilogy Golf Club in La Quinta, Sorenstam more than held her own. She holed a forty-yard bunker shot on the par-5 ninth hole for a winning eagle and $175,000 and then won the tenth hole to start the next day for another $50,000. She led the event at that point but finished second for the weekend behind—not surprisingly—Skins Game king Fred Couples. But Couples was more than impressed with Sorenstam's play.

"I think she played terrific golf," Couples said after the final putt. "I certainly didn't play better than Annika. I just made a few more putts and a couple of lucky shots."

Sorenstam was thirteenth in the 2004 Kraft Nabisco, merely mortal by her standards. But she won another official LPGA event in the Coachella Valley that same year. The Samsung World Championship, a limited-field event of just twenty players, was played at the Canyons Course at Bighorn Golf Club in Palm Desert, where Sorenstam happened to own property. The Canyons Course had made national headlines in 2000 when it hosted the Battle at Bighorn, an eighteen-hole match-play event between Tiger Woods and Sergio Garcia. ABC was to broadcast the event live in prime time to the East Coast, and lights were installed on the course to make sure the players and the television crews could see what was happening on the back nine. Garcia won the first Battle at Bighorn, but Woods teamed up with Sorenstam to win the 2001 event over David Duval and Karrie Webb. In 2002, the last Battle was won by Woods and Jack Nicklaus over Garcia and Lee Trevino.

Sorenstam won that 2004 Samsung title by three shots for a third desert win in four years. And she played again in the Skins Game, though she was not as big a factor as she had been the previous year.

Then came 2005 and a year few will ever match in the desert. At the Kraft Nabisco, Sorenstam broke open a tight tournament with a third-round 66 to take a 5-shot lead and then coasted home to an 8-shot victory for

Win the Masters, you get a green jacket. Win the Kraft Nabisco Championship, as Annika Sorenstam did three times, and you get a bathrobe. Here, Sorenstam celebrates her 2005 win, her third in the major championship. *Courtesy of International Management Group.*

The desert's LPGA tournament prided itself on showcasing the future of women's golf. Grace Park won the major title in 2006 but had played in the tournament as a college star as well. *Courtesy of International Management Group.*

her third Kraft title, tying Alcott and King for the most wins at Mission Hills. Six months later, it was a repeat performance at the Samsung World Championship at Bighorn. Sorenstam opened with a 64, shot 66 in the third round and won going away for another 8-shot victory. In five years, from 2001 through 2005, Sorenstam had won five official LPGA titles in the desert. It was all part of a career that included seventy-two wins and ten major titles before she retired in 2008 at the age of thirty-eight.

Sorenstam added a third Skins Game start in 2005, but that event is remembered less for her play or the fact that she and Woods were in the field together as for short-hitting Fred Funk donning a pink skirt when he was outdriven by Sorenstam on a hole on the front nine. The photos from Trilogy Golf Club rocketed around the world, but Funk had the last laugh by winning $925,000 of the $1 million purse.

While Sorenstam and the LPGA Tour rolled along, other tournaments struggled. The Skins Game had truly become a victim of its own success. Its ratings were dropping, its $1 million purse had been outpaced by regular PGA Tour events and other Silly Season events that the Skins Game had inspired and an increasing number of official tournaments around the world were popping up in the same general part of the year. That was making it tough to get a field of four great players like the Palmer-Nicklaus-Player-Watson days. After the 2008 event at the Indian Wells Golf Resort, the Skins Game faded away.

The Bob Hope Classic was finding tough times as well after its host passed away. Chrysler has been the title sponsor of the event since 1986, but the car manufacturer fell to the recession of the late 2000s, bankruptcy and the stigma of accepting federal bailout funds. Chrysler was one of several PGA Tour sponsors under pressure to not spend money on tour events while they were laying employees off and taking taxpayer bailouts. After the 2008 event, Chrysler was no long part of the event. Neither was comedian and actor George Lopez, who hosted the tournament in 2007 and 2008, perhaps an impossible job given he was following the greatest tournament host of all time in Hope.

From 2006 to 2008, the tournament added Classic Club in Palm Desert to the rotation, an Arnold Palmer course developed by the philanthropic Berger Foundation in Palm Desert and then given to Desert Classic Charities, the nonprofit that operates the tournament. But the course proved to be a bit polarizing, with some players saying the area north of the I-10 Freeway was too windy and others saying that the weather differences from one day to the next between Classic Club and courses fifteen miles

Even as Hope faded from the scene of his own tournament, big names continued to make news in the desert. One of those names was Phil Mickelson, who won the Hope title in 2002 and 2004. *Courtesy of Desert Classic Archives.*

away in La Quinta at PGA West were too great for a multicourse event. So in 2009, the tournament added the Nicklaus Private Course at PGA West to the four-course rotation. Classic Club was gone, Chrysler was gone and the tournament struggled for the next three years surviving on reserve funds and PGA Tour supplemental money while being unable to attract the top players in the game. It seemed like the tournament couldn't survive past 2012, if it made it that far at all.

But an old friend of the tournament became part of the salvation of the event. Former president Bill Clinton, who had famously played in the 1995 event with former presidents George H.W. Bush and Gerald Ford, was announced as part of a partnership with Humana, the PGA Tour and Desert Classic Charities. The Clinton Foundation would be part of a new agenda-based tournament that would promote health and wellness.

"I am pleased that my Foundation, which works to prevent childhood obesity in the United States and strengthen health systems across the globe, has partnered with Humana and the PGA Tour to promote wellness and carry on the legacy of Bob Hope and his tournament," Clinton said as the new partnership was announced.

For all the changes that have happened, there are some things that never changed in the Coachella Valley during the eight decades since the first few straggly golf holes popped up in the meadows at the Desert Inn in the mid-1920s. The Coachella Valley still attracts corporate giants, such as Phil Knight of Nike, Larry Ellsion of Oracle and Bill Gates of Microsoft, who all have part-time homes in the area. Ellison even owns his own backyard golf course, Porcupine Creek in Rancho Mirage. Presidents still escape to the desert for golf, including Bill Clinton, George W. Bush and Barack Obama. And celebrities still come to the desert for events like the ANA Inspiration (the new name of the Kraft Nabisco Championship as of 2015) and celebrity tournaments like the Frank Sinatra Invitational. And the best players in the world still come to the desert to play in big-money nationally televised events.

In those ways, people like Mother Coffman, Thomas O'Donnell, Helen Dettweiler, Johnny Dawson, Dwight Eisenhower, Dinah Shore and Bob Hope are still alive and well in the desert. They all helped to build the Coachella Valley into a golfing paradise, and their spirit is still alive on every fairway.

Index

About the Author

Larry Bohannan has been the golf writer and columnist for the *Desert Sun* newspaper and desertsun.com since 1986, covering the PGA Tour, LPGA and Champions Tour events in the Coachella Valley, as well as the rest of the desert golf scene from recreational to college golf. He has covered U.S. Opens, PGA Championships and other events in California. A 1982 graduate from Cal State Fullerton with a BA degree in communications, he was named the 2011

Photo by Marilyn Chung.

Media Person of the Year by the California Golf Writers and Broadcasters Association. He has previously authored *50 Years of Hope*, a history of the Bob Hope Classic. He lives in Indio.